WYETH CHRISTINA'S WORLD

LAURA HOPTMAN

THE MUSEUM OF MODERN ART, NEW YORK

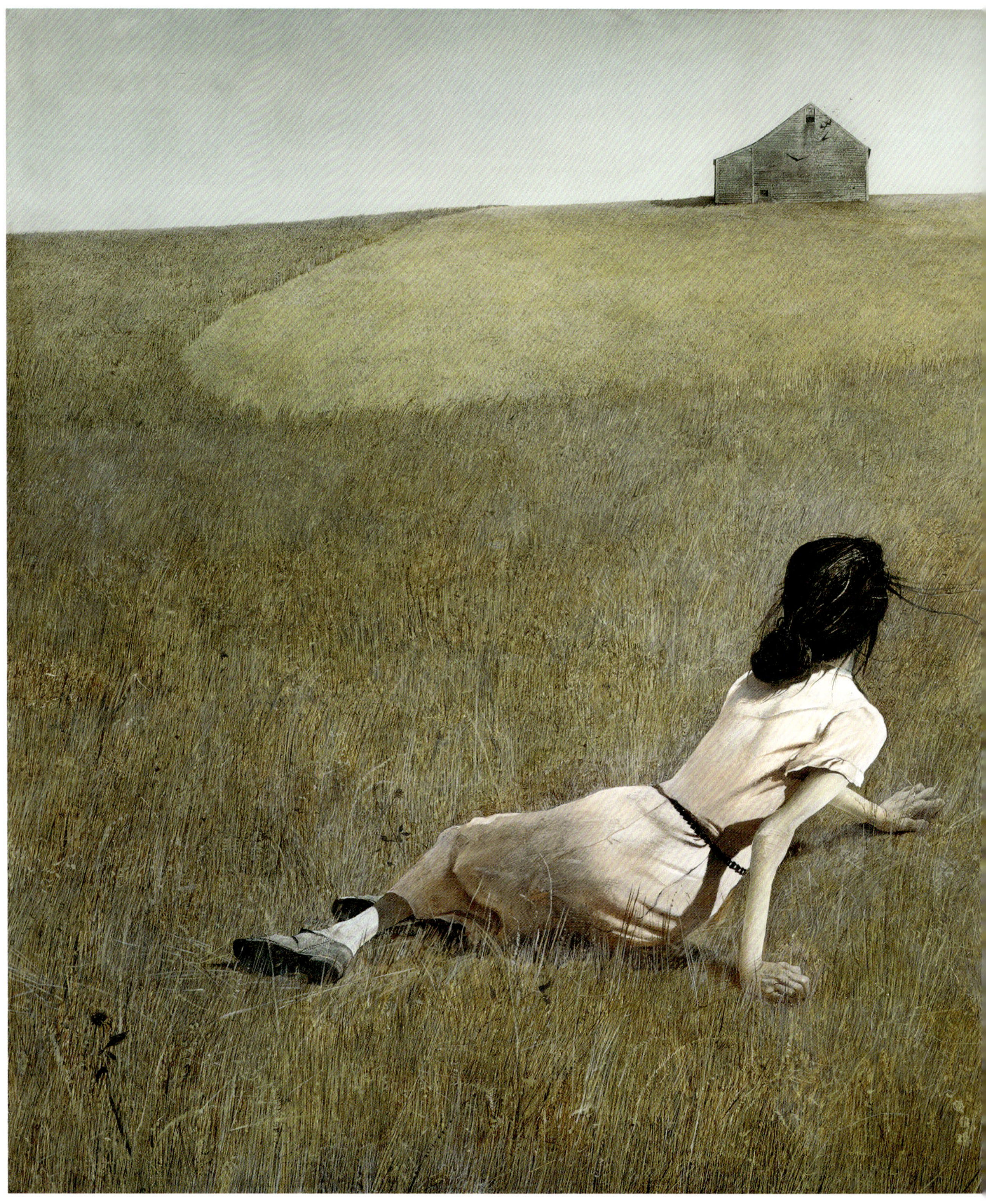

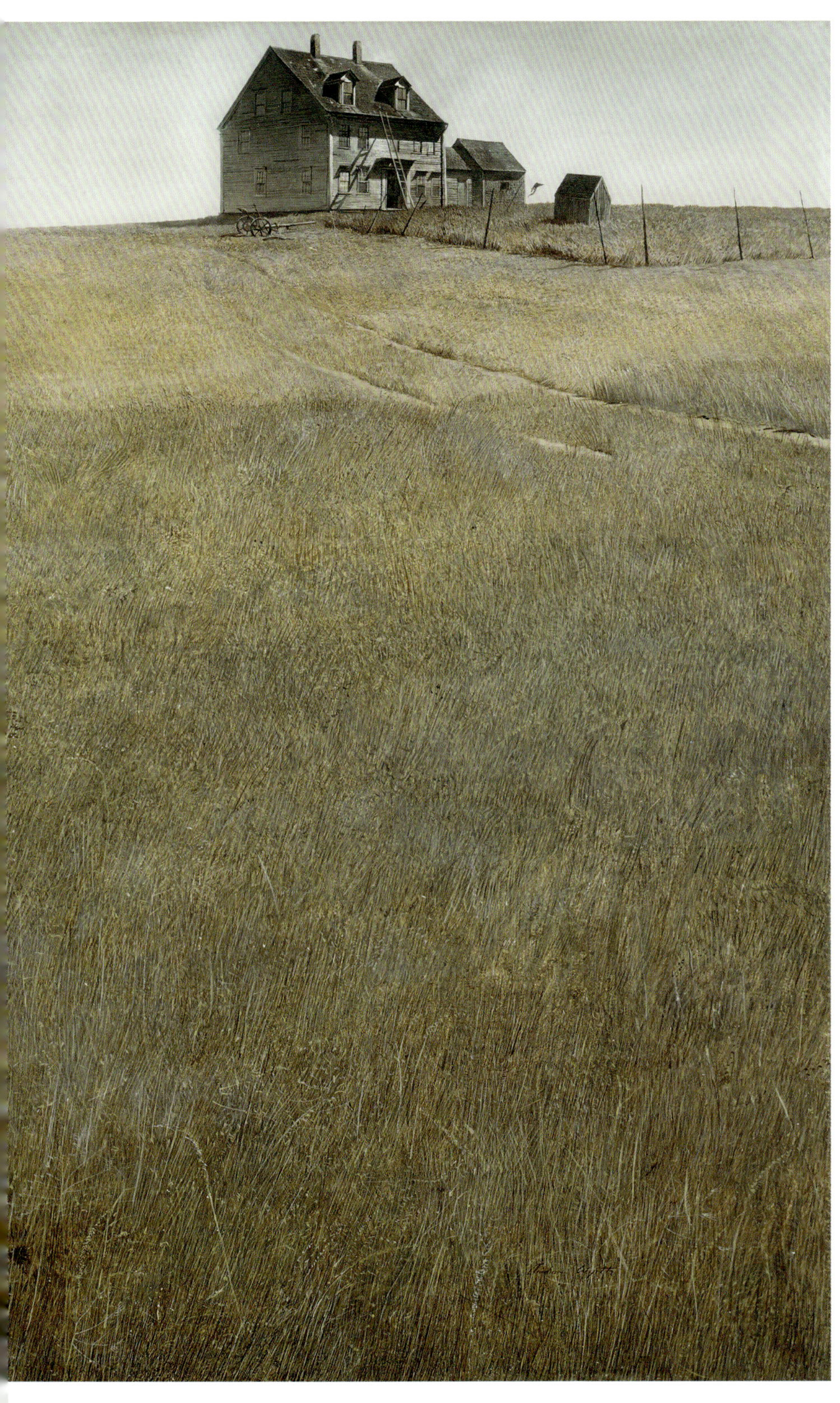

Andrew Wyeth (American, 1917–2009). *Christina's World.* 1948. Tempera on panel, 32¼ x 47¾" (81.9 x 121.3 cm). THE MUSEUM OF MODERN ART, NEW YORK. PURCHASE, 1949

WHEN ASKED BY A JOURNALIST IN 1977 TO NAME THE MOST UNDERRATED AND overrated artists in the history of art, the art historian Robert Rosenblum chose to submit one name for both categories: Andrew Wyeth.[1] Wyeth, an American realist painter whose life and career spanned the better part of the twentieth century, produced in 1948 one of the most iconic paintings in American art, a desolate Maine landscape with a single figure called *Christina's World*. This painting, acquired by The Museum of Modern Art in 1949, would become one of the most recognizable images in the history of American art, along with James Abbott McNeill Whistler's *Arrangement in Grey and Black No. 1 (Portrait of The Artist's Mother)* (1871; **FIG. 1**), better known as *Whistler's Mother*, and Grant Wood's *American Gothic* (1930; **FIG. 2**), a painting of a dour Midwestern farm couple in front of their homestead. *Christina's World* has been so widely reproduced that it has become a part of American popular culture, and it has also ignited heated arguments—about America's self-image, cultural parochialism, and taste—that added a measure of controversy to Wyeth's career, up to his death in 2009. Although controversies surrounding the role of Wyeth's work in American postwar art have shaped his artistic legacy, the popularity of the painting endures.

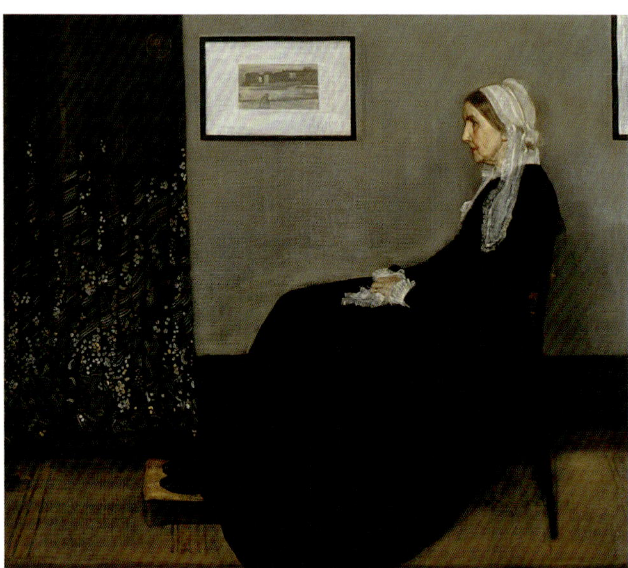

FIG. 1. James Abbott McNeill Whistler (American, 1834–1903). *Arrangement in Gray and Black No. 1 (The Artist's Mother)*. 1871. Oil on canvas, 56 13/16 x 64" (144.3 x 162.5 cm). MUSÉE D'ORSAY, PARIS

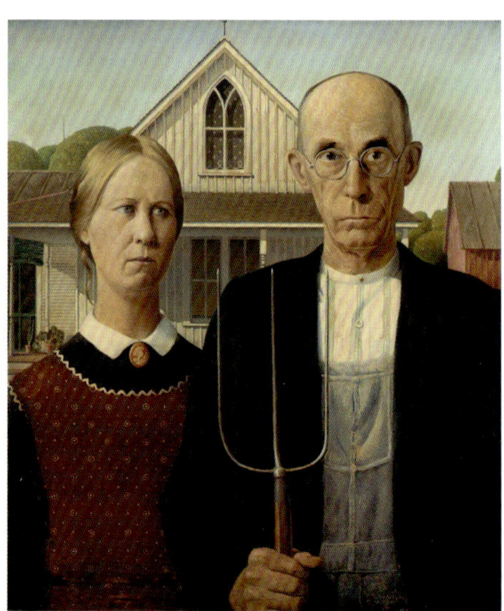

FIG. 2. Grant Wood (American, 1891–1942). *American Gothic*. 1930. Oil on beaver board, 30 3/4 x 25 3/4" (78 x 65.3 cm). THE ART INSTITUTE OF CHICAGO. FRIENDS OF AMERICAN ART COLLECTION

Christina's World is a modest-sized genre scene, painted in high detail with egg tempera on board. Set in the stark, barren landscape of coastal Maine, it depicts a young woman seen from behind, wearing a pink dress and lying in a mown field. Although she reclines gracefully, her upper torso, propped on her arms, is strangely alert; her silhouette is tense, almost frozen, giving the impression that she is fixed to the ground **[FIG. 3]**. Stock-still she stares, perhaps with longing, perhaps with fear, at a distant farmhouse and a group of outbuildings, ancient and grayed to harmonize with the dry grass and overcast sky. The scene is familiar, even picturesque, but it is also mysterious: Who is this young woman, vulnerable but also somehow indomitable? What is she staring at, or waiting for? And why is she lying in a field?

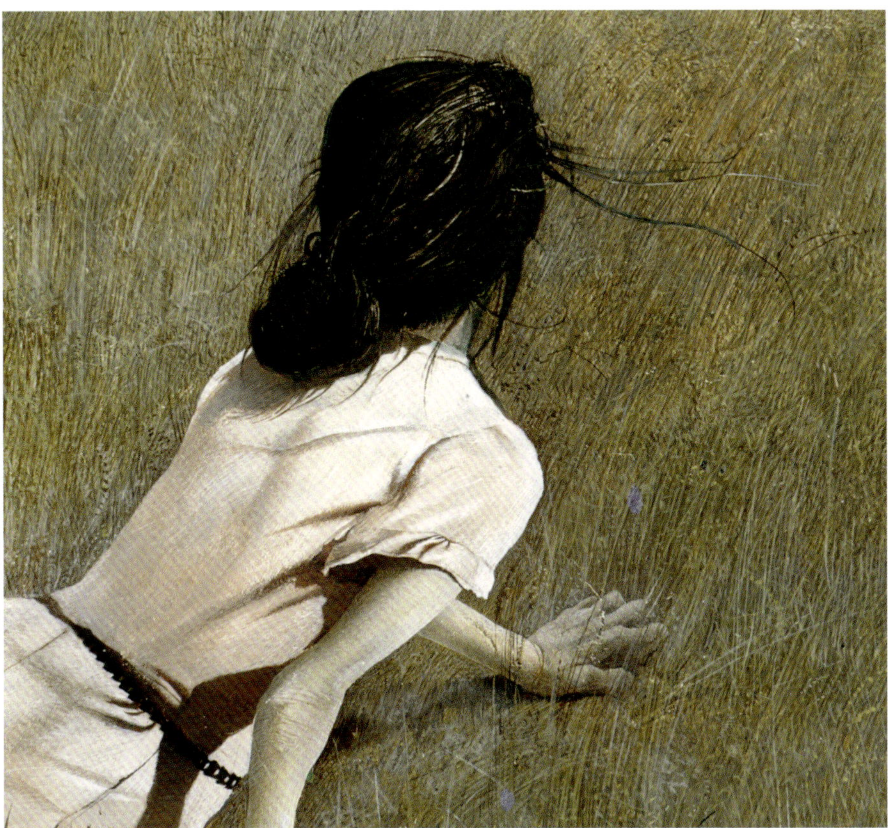

FIG. 3. Andrew Wyeth (American, 1917–2009). *Christina's World* (detail). 1948. See pp. 2–3

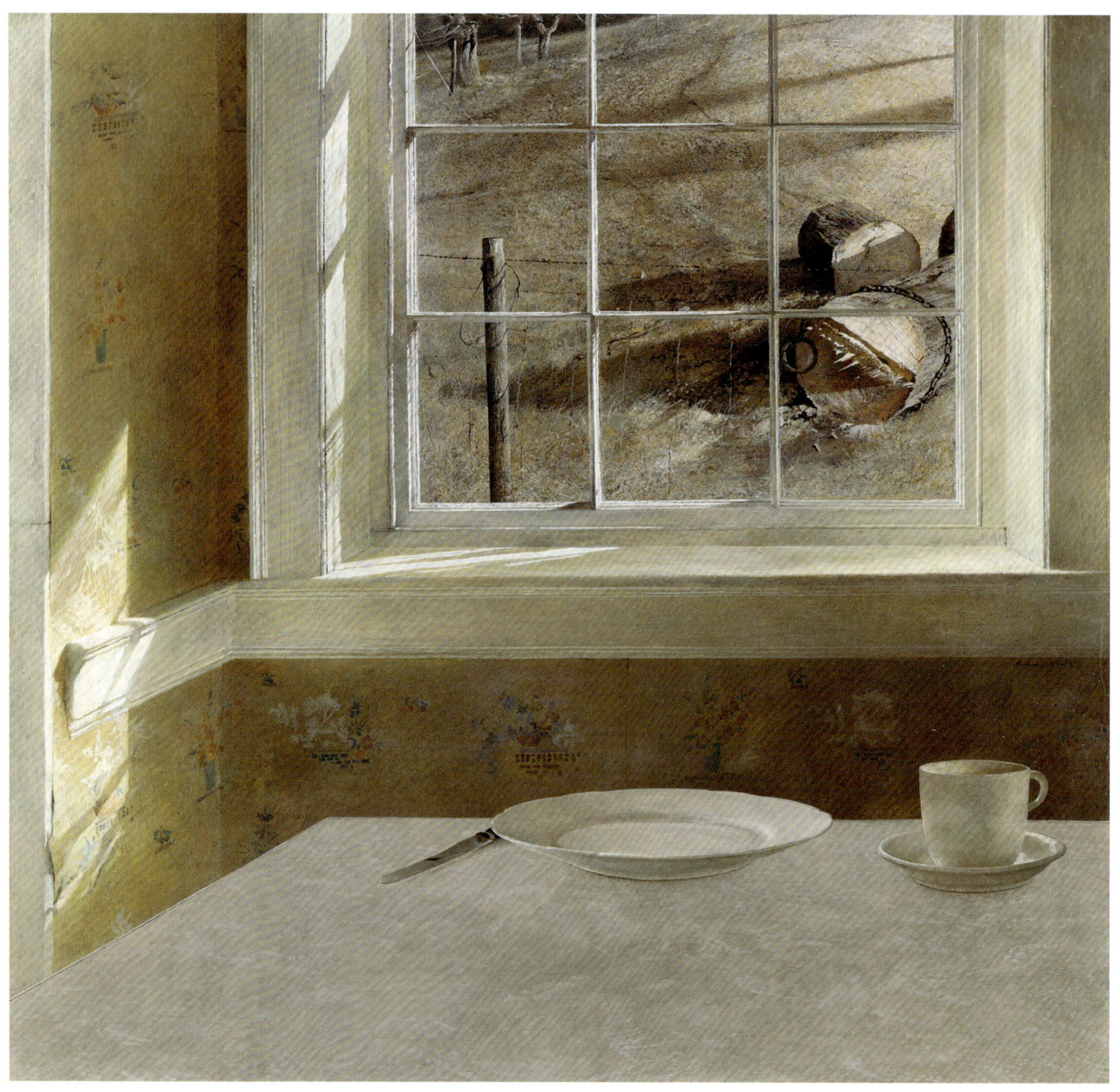

FIG. 4. Andrew Wyeth (American, 1917–2009). *Groundhog Day*. 1959. Tempera on panel, 31⅜ x 32⅛" (79.7 x 81.6 cm). PHILADELPHIA MUSEUM OF ART. GIFT OF HENRY F. DU PONT AND MRS. JOHN WINTERSTEEN

The painting was acquired by The Museum of Modern Art in 1949 for $1,800—a princely sum at the time—from the Macbeth Gallery on Fifty-seventh Street in New York City. Wyeth had exhibited his work there for almost a decade, and from his first solo exhibition, in 1937, he had attracted attention and achieved a good deal of financial success. The purchase of *Christina's World*, however, marked the beginning of a vertiginous rise in Wyeth's career. After its acquisition by the Museum, Wyeth was regularly featured in mainstream large-circulation magazines, such as *Time* and *Life*, during the 1950s and '60s and was hailed by these publications as America's most popular artist.[2] In 1959 his *Groundhog Day* (1959; **FIG. 4**) was purchased by the Philadelphia Museum of Art for thirty-five thousand dollars, the highest price ever paid by a museum for the work of a living American artist. In 1963 a midcareer retrospective of Wyeth's work at the Albright-Knox Art Gallery, in Buffalo, New York, attracted nearly 250,000 visitors—roughly half the population of the city. *Christina's World*, the show's centerpiece, provoked outpourings of emotion usually reserved for screen idols. One fan, from South Bend, Indiana, wrote plaintively to the museum, "I would so much like to see Mr. Wyeth's work. The two reproductions I saw in the paper have shaken me tremendously. I have even priced the railroad fare to your city but I'm afraid I can't make it. I have nine children, and little time and money to spare."[3]

Thanks in part to the sale of postcard and poster reproductions, *Christina's World* became so familiar that by the early 1960s it was also widely parodied, the lone figure gazing longingly at a distant goal cheerfully co-opted to sell everything from pale ale to air conditioners **[FIGS. 5 AND 6]**. A small industry sprang up around its subject, Anna Christina Olson, and her home, the farm in South Cushing, Maine, shown in the painting: after her death, in 1968, the house and

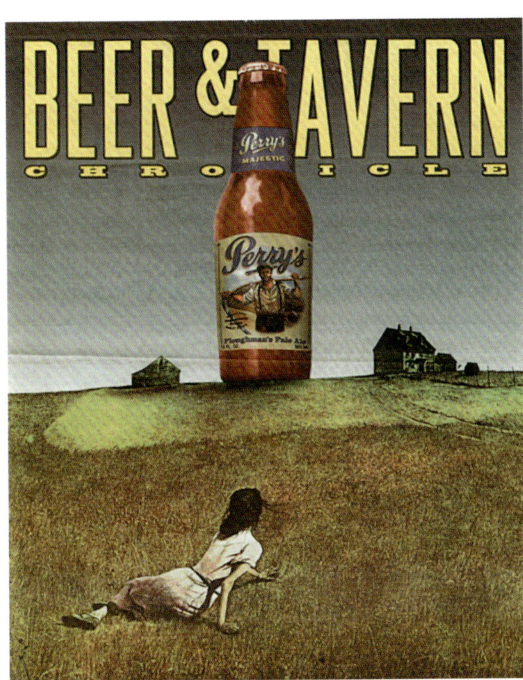

FIG. 5. Cover of *Beer & Tavern Chronicle*, April 1997

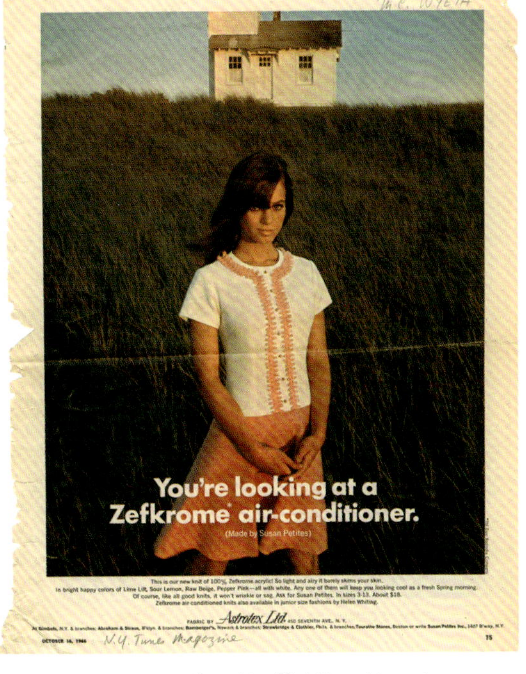

FIG. 6. Advertisement from *New York Times Magazine*, October 16, 1966

part of the property were purchased by a collector of Wyeth's work and restored with the intent of creating a Wyeth museum. The Olson House opened to the public in 1971 and was immediately swamped by Wyeth admirers who tramped across the property and plunked themselves down on the lawn Christina-style for a photograph against the famous backdrop. The site attracted so many visitors that the residents of South Cushing strongly protested, and the museum was closed barely a year after it opened. The Olson House reopened in 2000 under the aegis of the Farnsworth Art Museum, in Rockland, Maine, and is now on the National Register of Historic Places.

Wyeth first met Anna Christina Olson and her brother Alvaro in 1939, when she was forty-six years old. He was introduced by Betsy James, the woman who was to become his wife and whose family home was close to the Olson farm. *Christina's World* is the second of four tempera paintings of Christina that Wyeth completed from the time he met the Olsons until the siblings' deaths **[FIG. 7]**. He also made numerous drawings and watercolors of brother **[FIG. 8]**, sister, and house during his fifty years of friendship with the family.

A notable element of Wyeth's practice over his long career was his concentration on an extremely circumscribed number of subjects. In seventy years he painted the landscape, objects, and inhabitants of only two locations, never straying from his own neighborhoods: Chadds Ford, Pennsylvania, the village of his birth, and the area around the coastal village of South Cushing, where he had spent summers since early childhood. In the same way, Wyeth narrowed his focus to topics within these two geographical parameters, making lifelong subjects of families with whom he cultivated lasting relationships. The Olsons and the Kuerners, a German immigrant family in Chadds Ford, and the homes they inhabited and the farms they tended **[FIG. 9]**, became Wyeth's most frequent inspiration over his and their lifetimes. Wyeth became a fixture in those households (and several others), setting up studios in spare bedrooms and coming and going as he pleased, so that he became a fly-on-the-wall observer and recorder of the families' daily rituals. He painted Christina Olson and Karl Kuerner numerous times and became a close confidant of both **[FIGS. 10–12]**. A connoisseur of real-life entertainment before the advent of reality television, Wyeth made himself privy to his subjects' most private moments; in one painting he depicted two of his Chadds Ford friends sleeping, having come upon them very early one morning as he crept through their house **[FIG. 13]**.

FIG. 7. Andrew Wyeth (American, 1917–2009). *Christina Olson*. 1947. Tempera on panel, 33 x 25" (83.8 x 63.5 cm). CURTIS GALLERIES, MINNEAPOLIS

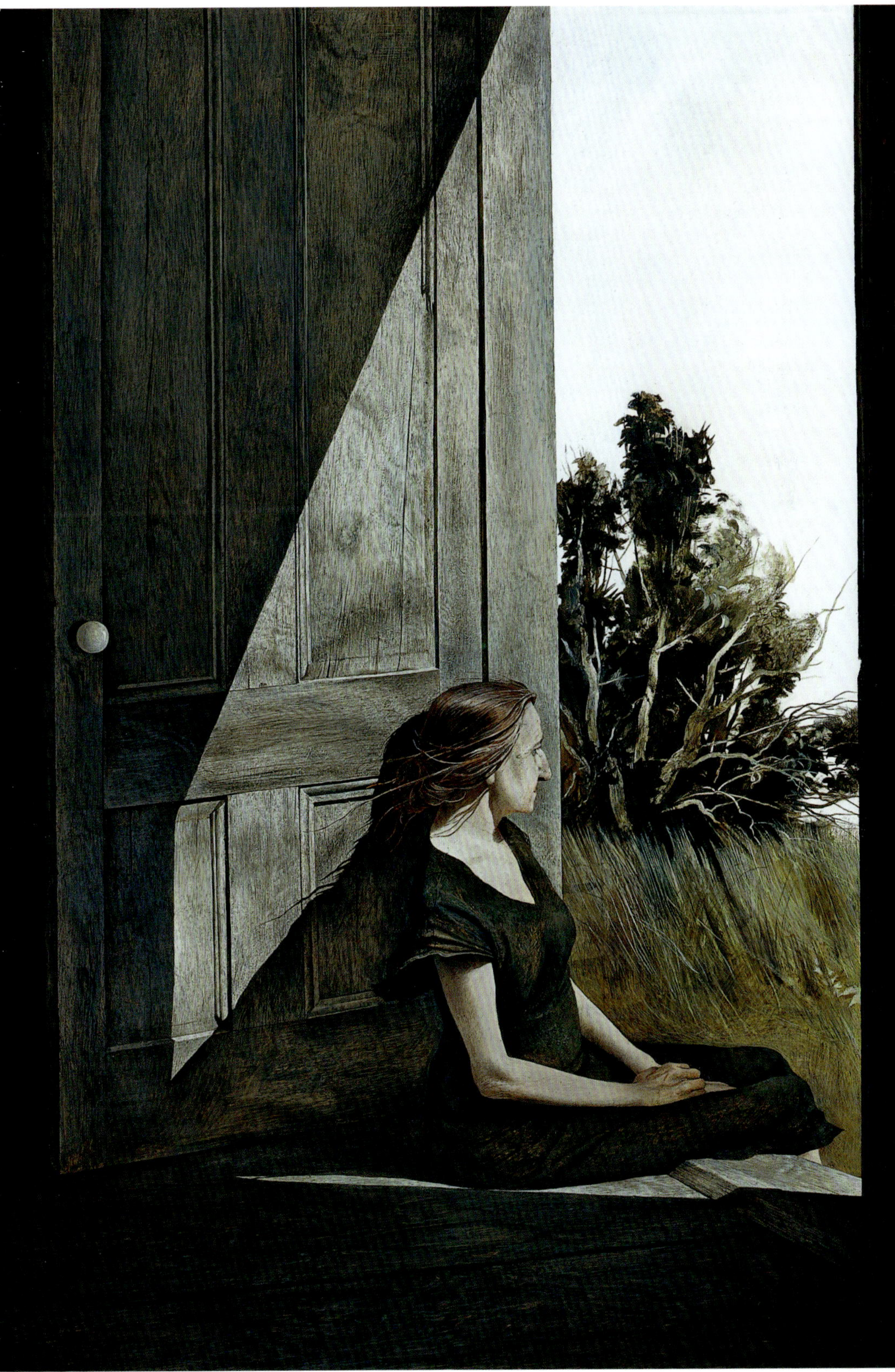

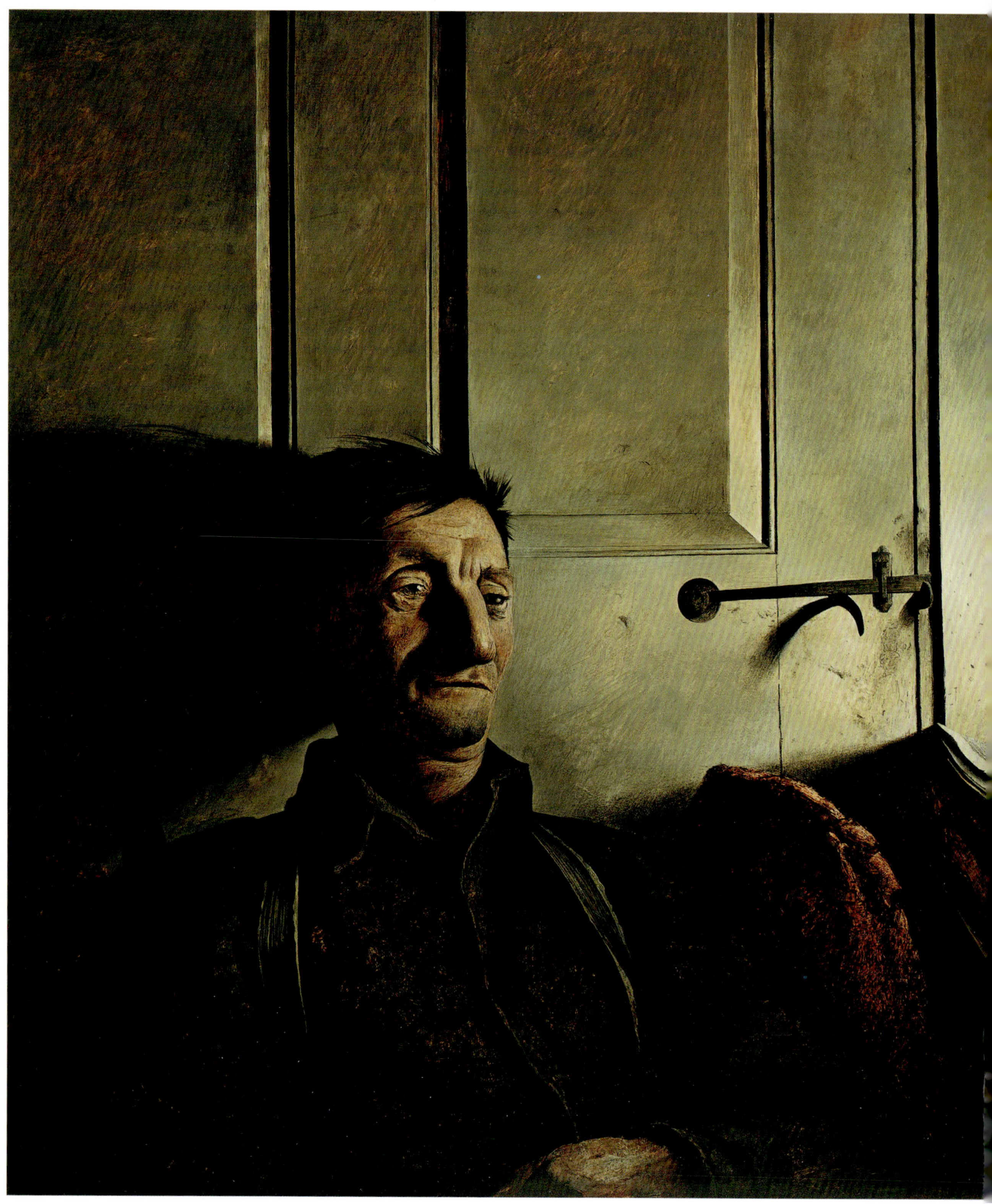

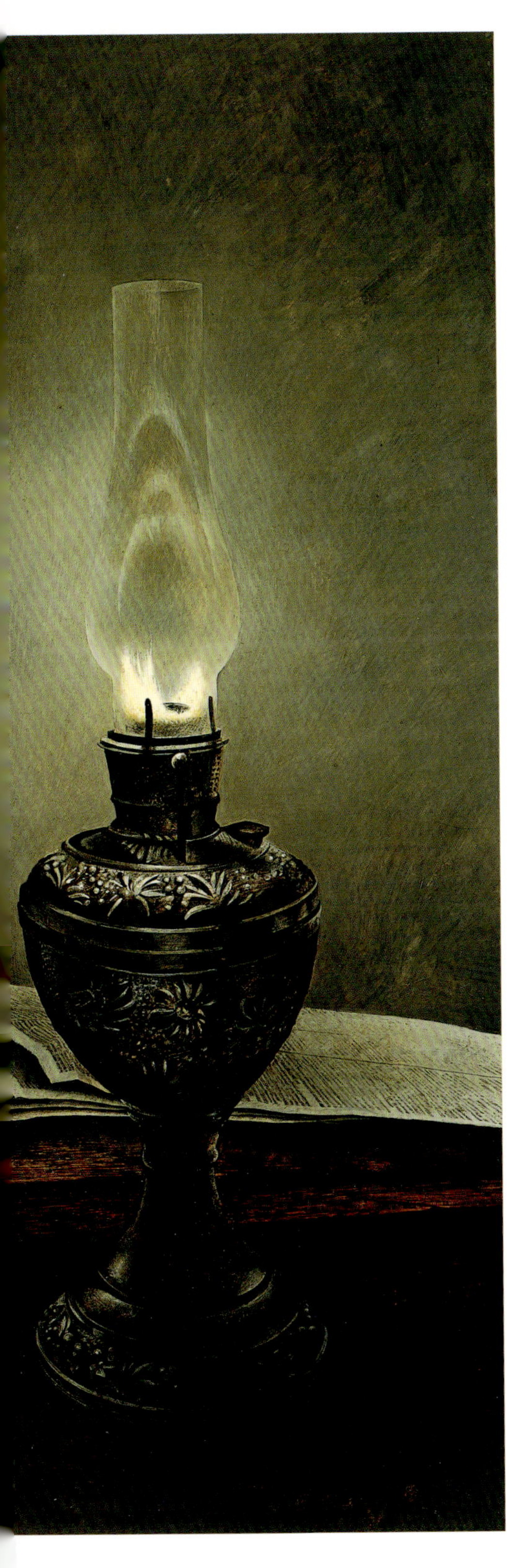

FIG. 8. Andrew Wyeth (American, 1917–2009). *Oil Lamp*. 1945. Tempera on panel, 34 x 42" (83.4 x 106.7 cm). WYETH COLLECTION

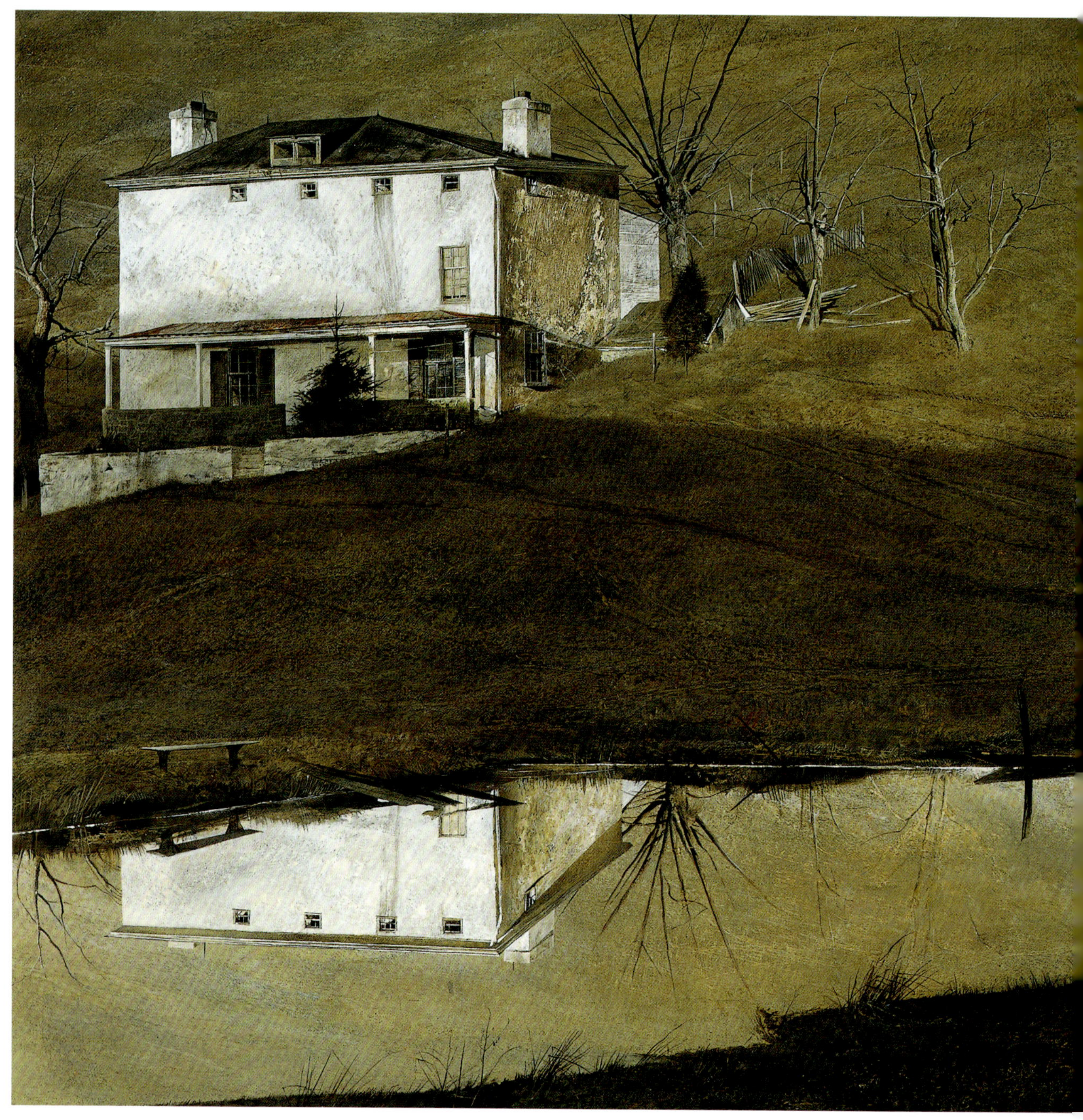

FIG. 9. Andrew Wyeth (American, 1917–2009). *Brown Swiss*. 1957. Tempera on panel, 30 x 60⅛" (76.2 x 152.7 cm). PRIVATE COLLECTION

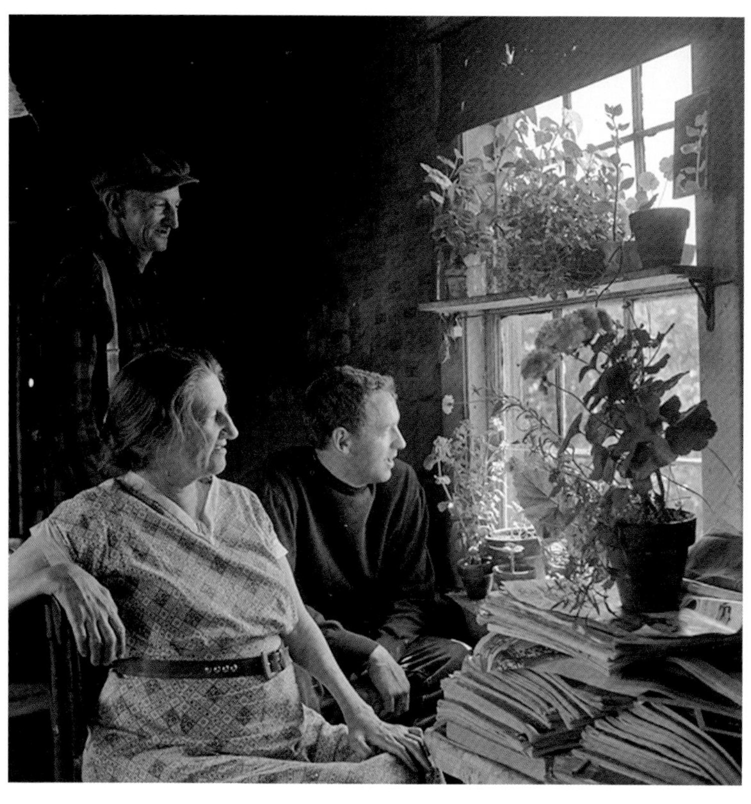

FIG. 10. Alvaro and Christina Olson and Andrew Wyeth, date unknown

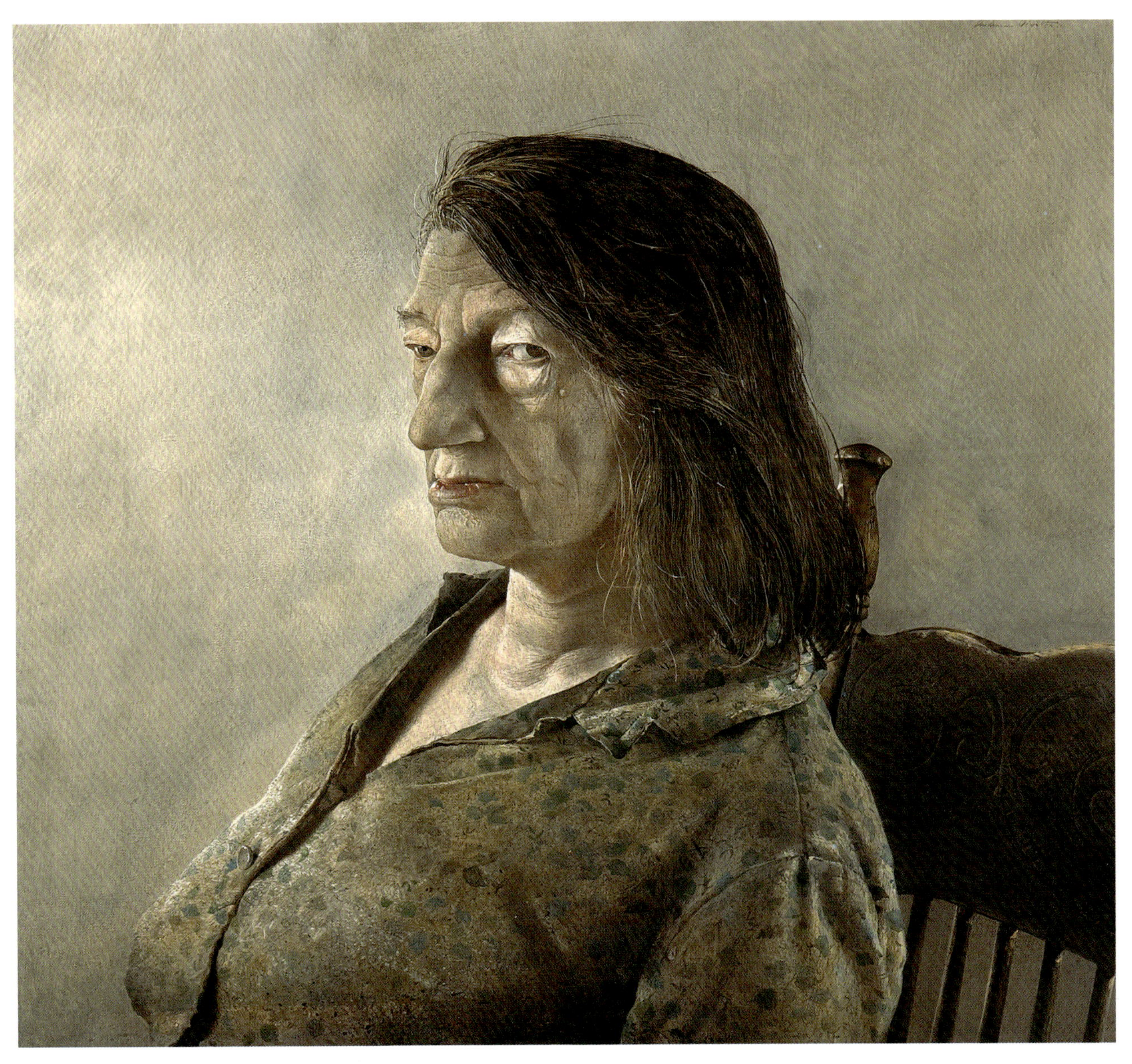

FIG. 11. Andrew Wyeth (American, 1917–2009). *Anna Christina*. 1967. Tempera on panel, 21¼ x 23½" (54 x 59.7 cm). BRANDYWINE RIVER MUSEUM, CHADDS FORD, PENNSYLVANIA, AND MUSEUM OF FINE ARTS, BOSTON. ANONYMOUS GIFTS

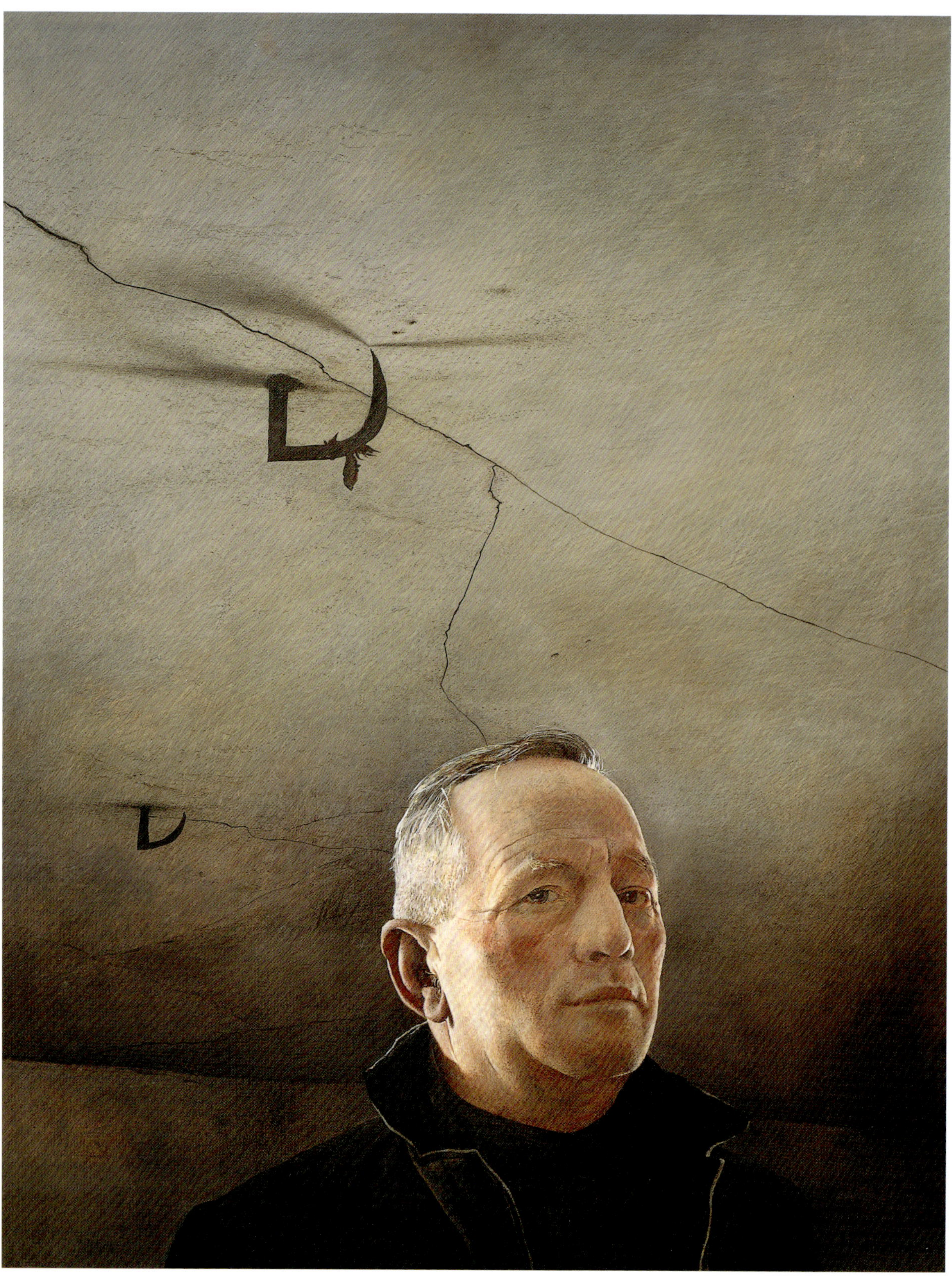

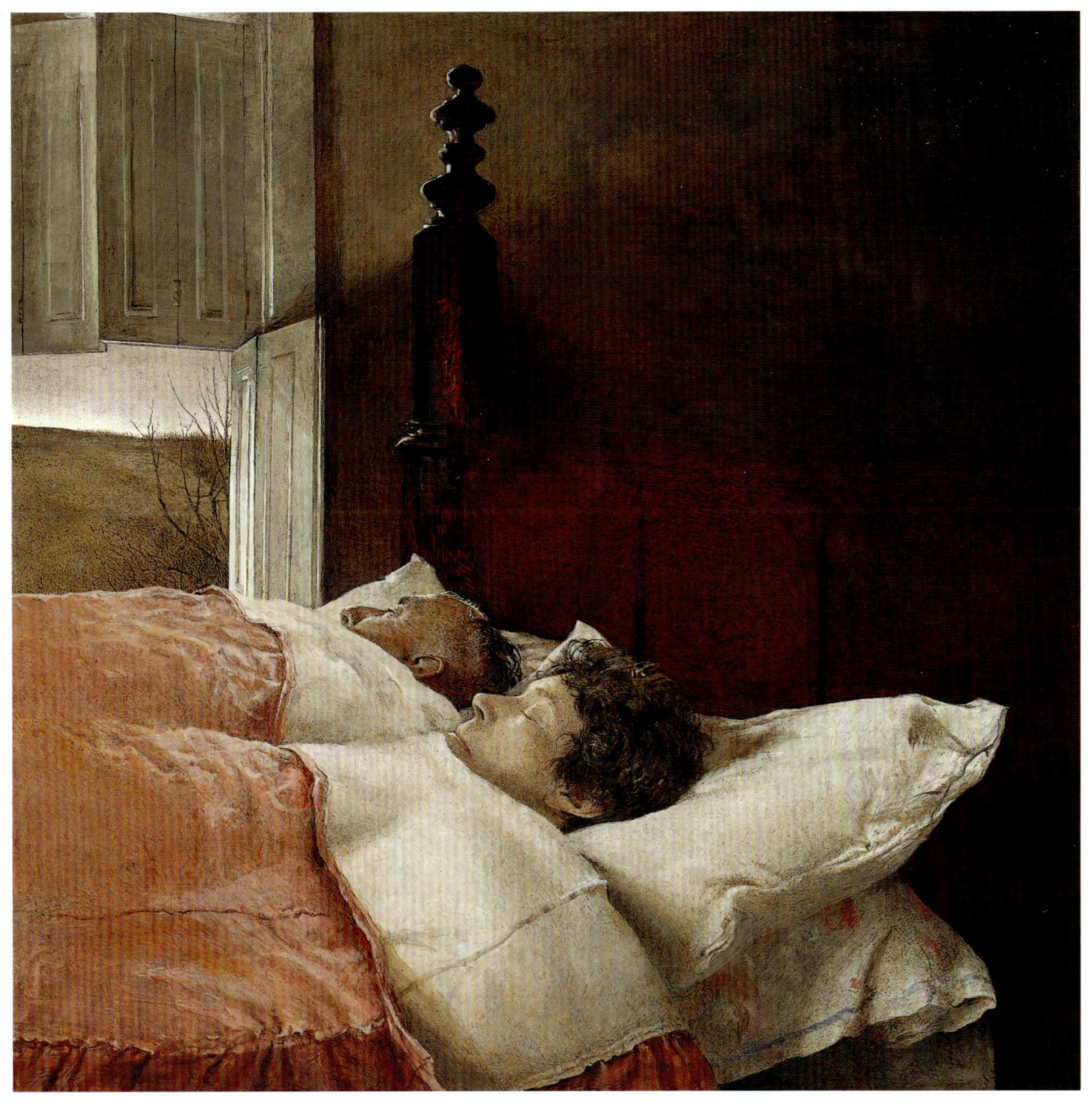

OPPOSITE: FIG. 12. Andrew Wyeth (American, 1917–2009). *Karl*. 1948. Tempera on panel, 30½ x 23½" (77.5 x 59.7 cm). PRIVATE COLLECTION

ABOVE: FIG. 13. Andrew Wyeth (American, 1917–2009). *Marriage*. 1993. Tempera on panel, 24 x 24" (61 x 61 cm). PRIVATE COLLECTION

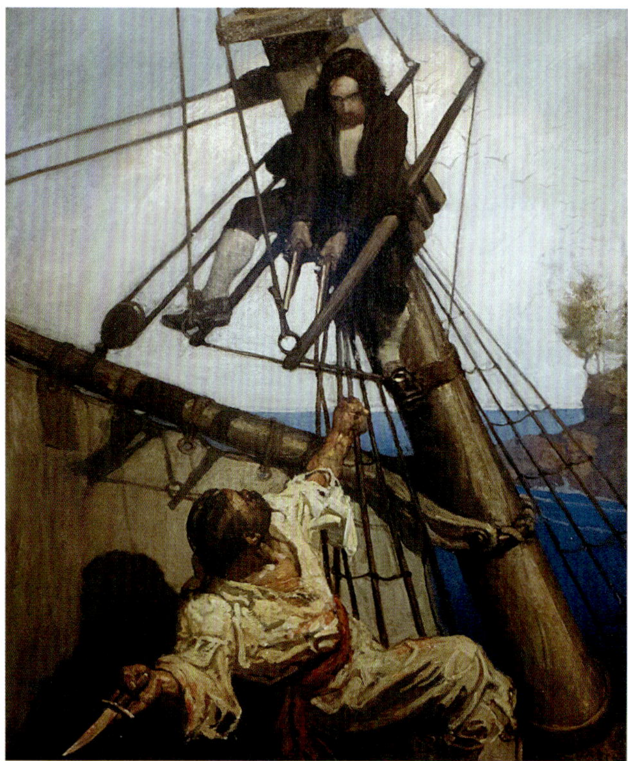

FIG. 14. N. C. Wyeth (American, 1882–1945). *"One more step, Mr. Hands," said I, "and I'll blow your brains out!,"* illustration for Robert Louis Stevenson's *Treasure Island* (New York: Charles Scribner's Sons). 1911. Oil on canvas, 47¼ x 38½" (120 x 97 cm). NEW BRITAIN MUSEUM OF AMERICAN ART, CONNECTICUT. HARRIET RUSSELL STANLEY FUND

Chadds Ford, a settlement on the banks of the Brandywine River, is less than fifteen miles from the bustling city of Wilmington, Delaware, and about twice that distance from Philadelphia, but it was still a rural community during Wyeth's lifetime. Wyeth's father, the well-known illustrator N. C. Wyeth **[FIG. 14]**, had moved to Chadds Ford from Massachusetts after studying with the illustrator Howard Pyle in Wilmington. When he finished his apprenticeship, he chose to remain there, and he built a house and studio where Wyeth learned to draw and paint. Wyeth was a sickly child and only briefly attended school. He was tutored at home and from the age of fifteen was apprenticed to his father, who led him through a rigorous curriculum that included studying masters such as Albrecht Dürer **[FIG. 15]** and drawing from plaster casts and eventually from live models, learning the kind of observation and draftsmanship that would lead him to develop his realistically precise mature style. Wyeth lived on or near the Chadds Ford compound where he was born for his entire life; when he and his wife moved off the family property in 1958, it was to a home only a mile and a half down the road.

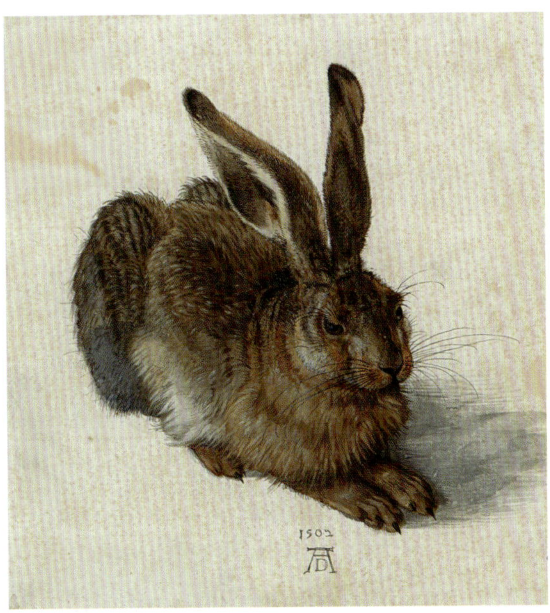

FIG. 15. Albrecht Dürer (German, 1471–1528). *Young Hare*. 1502. Gouache and watercolor on paper, 9⅞ x 8⅞" (25 x 22.5 cm).
ALBERTINA, VIENNA

His summers were spent in midcoastal Maine—in his parents' house in Port Clyde as a child, and after his marriage in his own home nearby, on the property of Betsy Wyeth's family in the tiny hamlet of South Cushing. South Cushing was at midcentury primarily home to New England families, mostly fisherman and hardscrabble farmers, who had been there for generations. Christina Olson was descended on her mother's side from the Hathorns of Salem, Massachusetts, an old New England family related to John Hathorn, the chief judge at the Salem witch trials. The house in Wyeth's painting, known as Hathorn House, was built for the family in 1801 and turned into a boarding house in 1871. Her father was a Swedish seaman whose boat was stranded one winter in the ice off the Maine coast; he met her mother and decided to stay.

As a young girl, Christina developed a degenerative muscle condition—possibly polio—that robbed her of the use of her legs by the time she was in her early thirties. One of four children, she never married but stayed in the house with her unmarried brother, Alvaro, and her father for the rest of her life. Although handicapped and meagerly supported by her brother's small-scale subsistence farming, Christina was a visible part of her South Cushing community and did not appear to be an object of pity. She refused to use a wheel chair, preferring to scoot herself across the floor in a kitchen chair or, when outside, to crawl, using her arms to drag her lower body along.

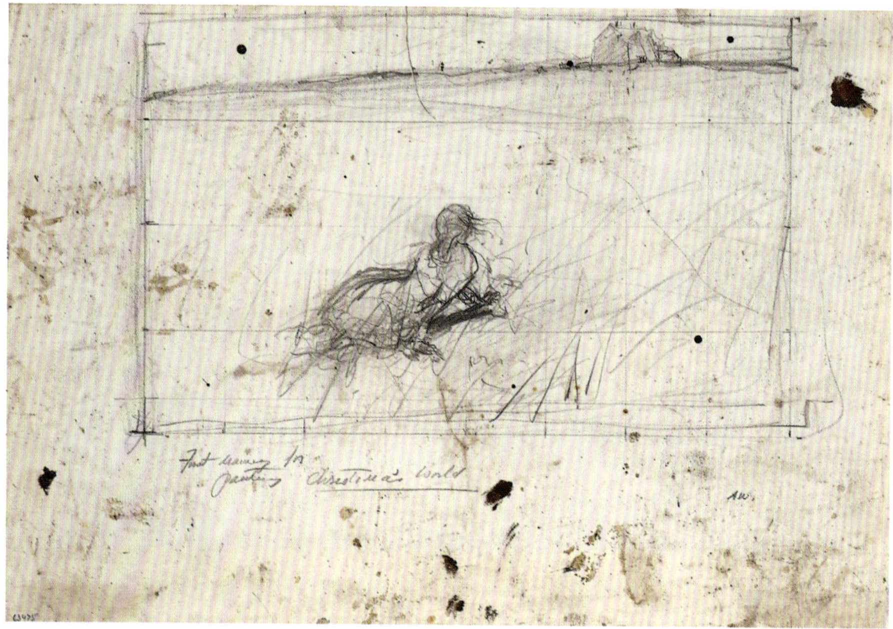

FIG. 16. Andrew Wyeth (American, 1917–2009). Study for *Christina's World*. 1948. Pencil on paper, 12 x 18¾" (30.5 x 47.6 cm). COLLECTION MARUNUMA ART PARK, ASAKA, JAPAN

Wyeth was inspired to paint *Christina's World* when he happened to observe Christina making her way up a hill after picking vegetables from the family garden. He was in the studio he had set up in an unused bedroom on the third floor of the Olson home, the large clapboard house seen in the painting at the top of the hill, and although he had a bird's-eye view of Christina, he chose to paint her from the reverse perspective, with Hathorn House in the background. This choice of a worm's-eye view, which sites the viewer slightly below a looming Christina, does two important things: it places us virtually in the grass alongside her, almost encouraging us to join her uphill struggle, and it allowed Wyeth to indulge in what his chosen medium and tools—tempera applied with tiny brushes—do best: the rendering of minute detail.

Wyeth began painting *Christina's World* in May 1948 and completed it in September of the same year. After making a quick pencil drawing that included all of the painting's main compositional elements **[FIG. 16]**, he started the background on a Masonite board covered with gesso, a primer made of rabbit-skin glue and white clay. On top of the gesso, he used egg tempera, a painting material used as far back as the Middle Ages, which he had learned to make from his brother-in-law, the painter Peter Hurd. Egg tempera consists of powdered pigment combined with egg yolk and distilled water; when it dries, it creates a hard and very durable surface. Wyeth used extremely thin brushes, some with

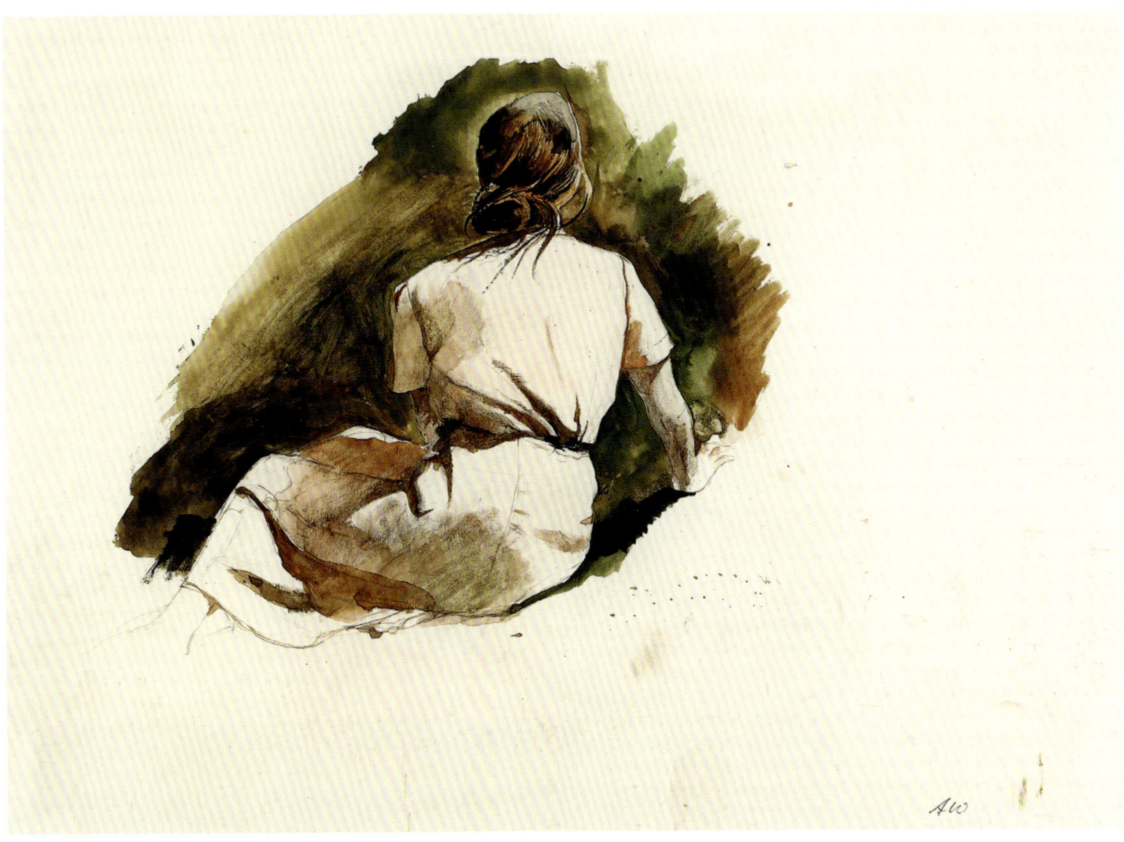

FIG. 17. Andrew Wyeth (American, 1917–2009). Study for *Christina's World.* 1948. Watercolor, 14½ x 20" (36.8 x 50.8 cm). COLLECTION MARUNUMA ART PARK, ASAKA, JAPAN

only several hairs, and these, together with the tempera medium, which is less viscous than the linseed oil used in oil painting, allowed him to draw with paint with precision and delicacy. At the time of the painting Christina was in her mid-fifties, paraplegic, and weathered-looking, but Wyeth transformed her into a much younger, more winsome figure by faithfully reproducing only two elements of the real woman: her rickety arms and pink housedress. The rest of the figure depicted is the lithe body of his twenty-six-year-old wife **[FIG. 17]**. Christina's face is turned away from the viewer in an effect called a "lost profile," which obscures her features completely, something that disappointed Christina when she saw the work for the first time but which allows scope for a viewer's imagination and reinforces the timeless quality of the image.[4] If the figure of Christina is fascinating in its specificity, encouraging our curiosity about her identity and the details of her life, it is also deeply enigmatic. For all the detail that the artist provides, his Christina is less a picture of a living individual than an allegorical figure of American womanhood.

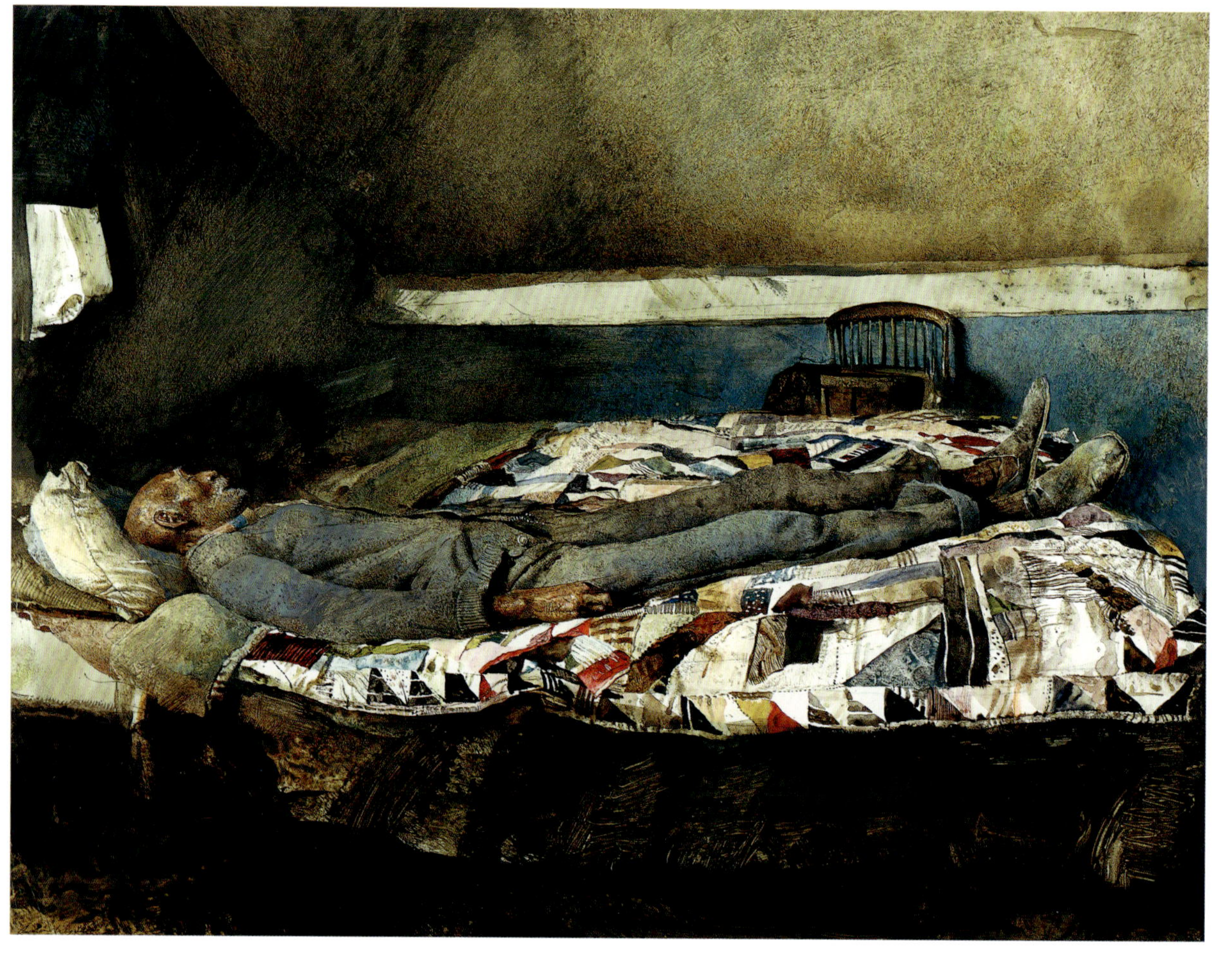

FIG. 18. Andrew Wyeth (American, 1917–2009). *Garret Room*. 1962. Drybrush on paper, 18 x 23" (45.7 x 58.4 cm). PRIVATE COLLECTION

In an article written for *Art News* in 1950, the painter Elaine de Kooning noted that Wyeth first drew the background composition of his works and then painted in one area at a time, adding individual motifs in much the same way one completes a jigsaw puzzle. However central the figure of Christina seems to us to be, in Wyeth's account he did not begin with the figure but added it as the painting's final element. In preparation he posed Christina in the grass and made studies of her skinny arms with their swollen joints and gnarled hands. "When I put (these details) on paper," he recalled, "my cold eye took in the deformity and it shook me."[5] Throughout his career Wyeth was drawn to subjects with physical or mental handicaps or suffering from disadvantages such as poverty **[FIG. 18]**. He was fascinated with Christina's disabilities, describing her as "crab-like" and a "wounded gull."[6] But he also recognized that the potency of her deformities could overshadow his metaphorical depiction of her indomitability, which may be why he chose not to overtly portray her condition. That Christina cannot walk is not apparent to the viewer, although it is suggested in the way she props herself up with her unhealthy-looking arms and arthritic hands, which seem to claw the ground as if trying to stabilize her torso **[FIG. 19]**.

In a letter to Alfred H. Barr, Jr., The Museum of Modern Art's director, written soon after the Museum purchased the painting, Wyeth explained that his aim in *Christina's World* was not to picture physical limitations but to convey the challenge of limitless possibilities. "Miss Olson is a personal friend—her physical limitations are appalling," he wrote. "The challenge to me was to do justice to her extraordinary conquest of a life which most people would consider hopeless. If in some small way I have been able in paint to make the viewer sense that her world may be limited physically but by no means spiritually, then I have achieved what I set out to do."[7] Regarding the work's title he wrote, "*Christina's World* is, because of her physical handicap, outwardly limited—but in this painting I tried to convey how unlimited it really is."[8]

The figure of Christina is the central element in a painting in which every detail contributes to this idea: the grandeur that can be found in a life radically

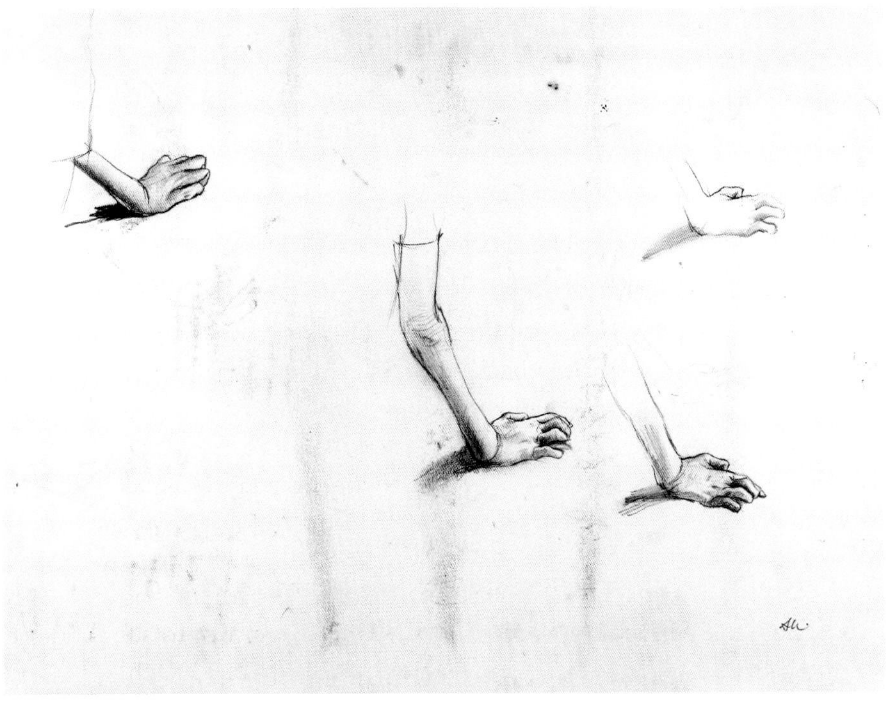

FIG. 19. Andrew Wyeth (American, 1917–2009). Study for *Christina's World*. 1948. Pencil, 15 x 22" (38.1 x 55.9 cm). COLLECTION MARUNUMA ART PARK, ASAKA, JAPAN

circumscribed by place and situation. With her yearning pose and her anonymity, the figure powerfully conveys a mood reinforced by virtually all the other elements in the painting. As in all of Wyeth's works, details—such as a piece of clapboard siding **[FIG. 20]** or the strangely fashionable brown lace-up shoes that Christina wears—are rendered with a specificity that almost lends them personalities. They are more than atmospheric props; they play parts in the stories that his paintings tell and are almost equal in importance to the people he depicts. *Christina's World* evokes a vast emptiness that is both limitless and lonely not only with its solitary figure but also with the almost endless expanse of dead grass, unrelieved by weeds or stumps. The feeling is magnified by the details in the distance: the apparently abandoned house, the tiny pair of unclaimed britches on a clothesline deep in the background. Wyeth declared in a number of interviews, not altogether facetiously, that despite Christina's central role, her figure might well be a superfluous detail in the painting; he claimed that had he left her out completely, the painting would have conveyed the same sense of isolation and longing.[9] In a later painting he did just that; *Alvaro and Christina* (1968; **FIG. 21**) is a portrait of the two Olson siblings but features only two old doors from the Olson house standing side by side, one blue, the other white. For Wyeth the rough, weather-beaten character of these two inanimate objects embodied his two friends just as well as their likenesses would have.

The high level of detail Wyeth gave to every object in his paintings encourages intense inspection, even contemplation, but it is his titles that reveal the inner significance of the outwardly mundane objects that make up his compositions. The title *Christina's World*, courtesy of Wyeth's wife, Betsy, indicates that the painting is more a psychological landscape than a portrait, a portrayal of a state of mind rather than a place. Rather than the straightforward, realistic depic-

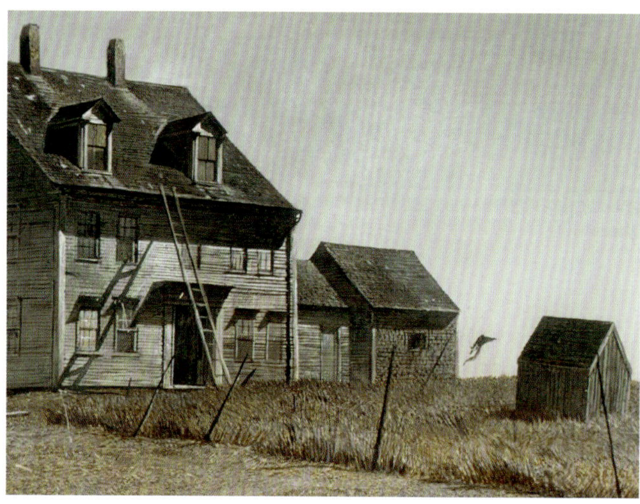

FIG. 20. Andrew Wyeth (American, 1917–2009). *Christina's World* (detail). 1948. See pp. 2–3

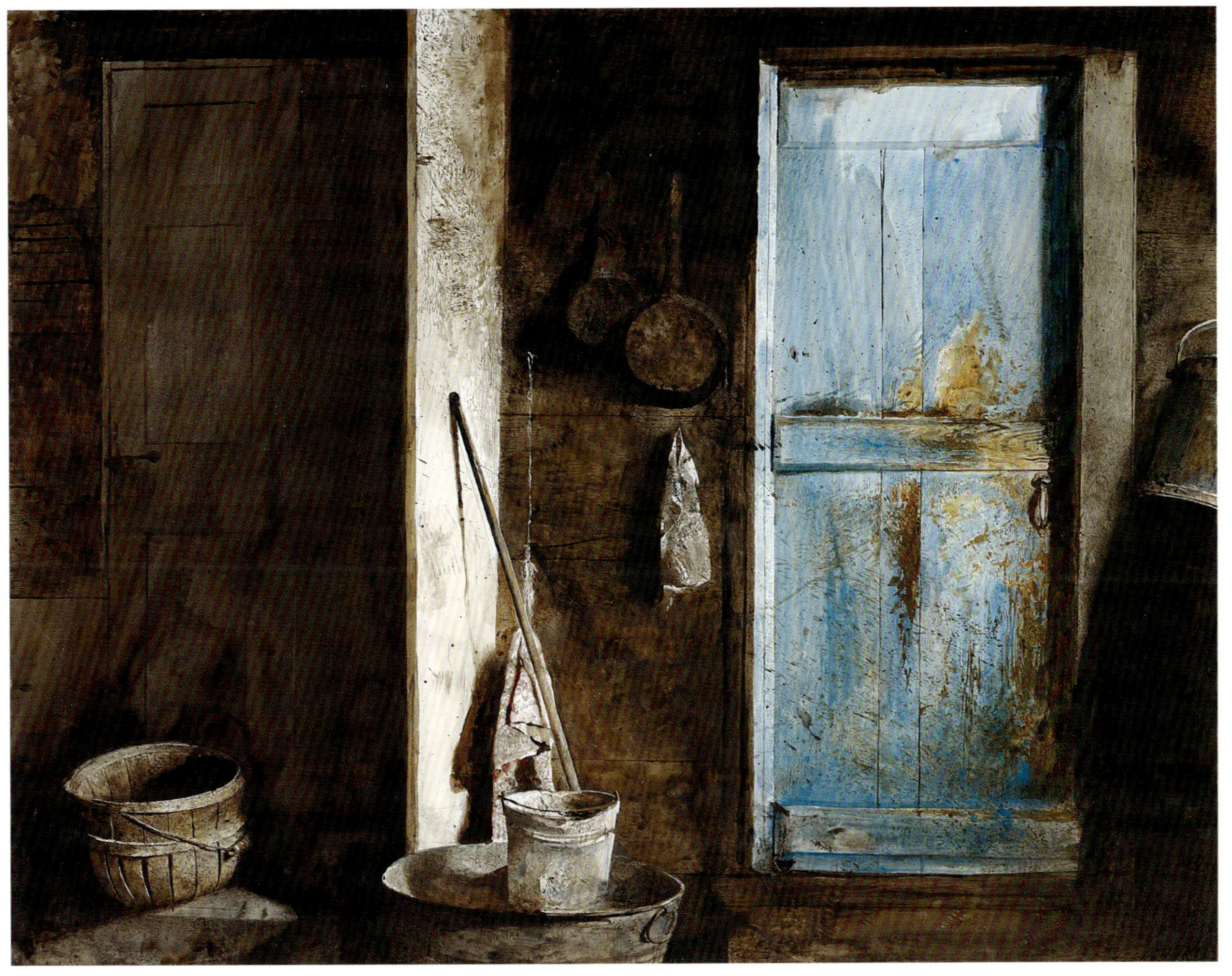

FIG. 21. Andrew Wyeth (American, 1917–2009). *Alvaro and Christina*. 1968. Watercolor on paper, 22 13/16 x 28 3/4" (57.9 x 73 cm). FARNSWORTH ART MUSEUM, ROCKLAND, MAINE. MUSEUM PURCHASE

tion it appears to be, it is a provocative mixture of observation and imagination, from Christina's rather startling combination of girlish beauty and grotesque disfigurement to the vast meadow where she has been marooned, which in reality is a modest stretch of lawn between a house and a vegetable garden. As Wyeth's career progressed, the elision of carefully observed naturalism with fantasy would become increasingly important to his work.

Wyeth had exhibited regularly at Macbeth, which was known for its stable of American realist painters, including Winslow Homer and Edward Hopper **[FIG. 22]**, and had built his reputation with museums and collectors of American art as a part of that tradition. But he did not wear the realist or regionalist mantles lightly, periodically even flatly rejecting them. In a 1963 profile in *Time*

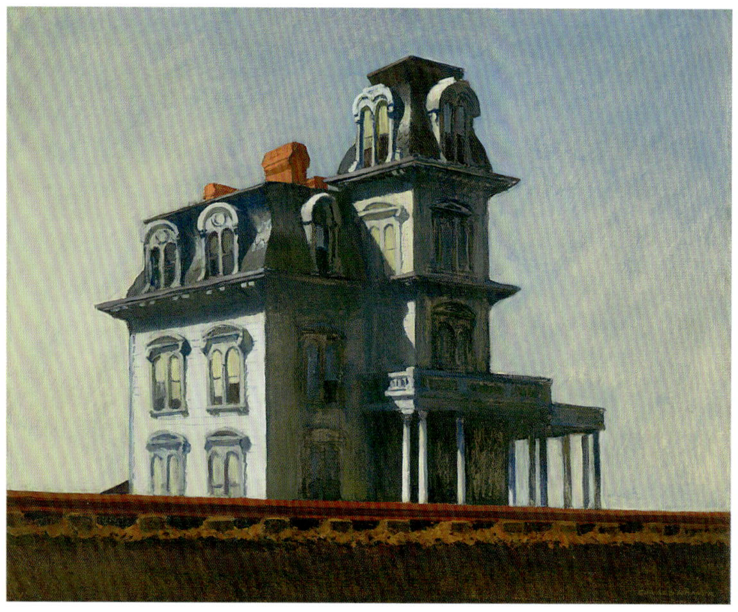

FIG. 22. Edward Hopper (American, 1882–1967). *House by the Railroad*. 1925. Oil on canvas, 24 x 29" (61 x 73.7 cm). THE MUSEUM OF MODERN ART, NEW YORK. GIVEN ANONYMOUSLY, 1930

magazine, he provocatively proclaimed, "I'm no more like a realist, such as [Thomas] Eakins or [John Singleton] Copley than I'm like the man in the moon."[10] Indeed, his hyperdetailed but fundamentally idealized landscapes seem far from the immediacy and anecdotal naturalism of those painters. Rendered in a palette of close color values that gives them a dry, airless quality and a dead, unnatural stillness, they present scenes quite the opposite of the living, buzzing natural world rendered in the atmospheric oil paintings of nineteenth-century realists such as Eakins. Wyeth's work at the end of the 1930s can be more fruitfully compared with that of the American Scene painters such as Wood, Thomas Hart Benton, and John Steuart Curry, who, during the Depression, concentrated on subjects specific to American life but depicted them idealistically, grandly, even fantastically, in a timeless, allegorical way, as Ansel Adams did in his photographs, Robert Frost did in his poems, and Aaron Copland did in his music. During the 1930s, naturalistic realism and American Scene realism existed simultaneously and were equally prominent in the American art world, which was known for its realist tradition stretching back to the country's founding.

Wyeth's painting was an interesting purchase for The Museum of Modern Art, which in 1949 was best known for its groundbreaking exhibitions of avant-garde European artists such as Pablo Picasso and Henri Matisse. However, MoMA's focus on the newest stylistic trends and innovations included the currents of American art in the 1930s and 1940s; its curators did not confine themselves to European avant-gardists but purchased paintings for the collection by American figurative painters such as Charles Sheeler, Wood, Benton, Ben Shahn, and Hopper. In 1943, five years before Wyeth painted *Christina's World*, five of his paintings and three drawings were included in *American Realists and Magic Realists*, an important group exhibition of contemporary art organized by Barr and curator Dorothy C. Miller. Barr and Miller had first seen a tempera painting by Wyeth at an exhibition at the Corcoran Gallery of Art in Washington, D.C., earlier that year. They were impressed enough to inquire about it but, put off by its price, did not purchase it. They did, however, include it in their exhibition.

American Realists and Magic Realists gathered paintings and drawings by twenty-six painters of Wyeth's generation, all working in what the curators defined as an American realist tradition of sharply focused and precise representations of objects and figures, painted with "a termite gusto for detail."[11] Without directly mentioning the United States' involvement in World War II and the attendant surge of patriotism that permeated American popular culture, Miller argued in the exhibition catalogue that realism reflected American values in its ability to communicate to a wide range of viewers. "No other style of painting appeals so naturally to the great majority of people," she wrote, "and in this sense it is a truly democratic style, offering no barrier of technique between the artist and the untrained eye."[12] The exhibition began with a retrospective look at American realism with still lifes by eighteenth- and nineteenth-century practioners such as Raphaelle Peale and trompe l'oeil still life painter William Harnett; a painting of the ivory-billed woodpecker by John James Audubon; landscapes by Thomas Cole and Homer; the *Peaceable Kingdom* (c. 1834), by the folk painter Edward Hicks; and *Max Schmitt in a Single Scull* (1871; **FIG. 23**), the great portrait-and-landscape combination by Eakins, among other well-known American masterpieces. In order to emphasize their importance to Wyeth's generation of painters, Hopper and Sheeler were represented by several works each. Their coldly lit urban landscapes, at once precise and imaginary, were referred to in the catalogue as examples of "the Frigidaire school" and cited as direct influences on the more recent work in the exhibition.[13]

The group of contemporary works assembled by Miller and Barr included realists, who painted observable subjects, and magic realists **[FIG. 24]**, defined by Barr as painters "who by means of an exact realistic technique try to make plausible and convincing their improbable, dreamlike or fantastic visions."[14] The exhibition catalogue did not divide the artists into two categories, but rather indicated that these designations were two points on a continuum along which participating artists fell. Wyeth's *Winter Fields* (1942; **FIG. 25**), for example, compared in its "Schubertian purity" to the work of German Romantic painter Caspar David Friedrich, exhibited characteristics of both styles.[15] The exactitude

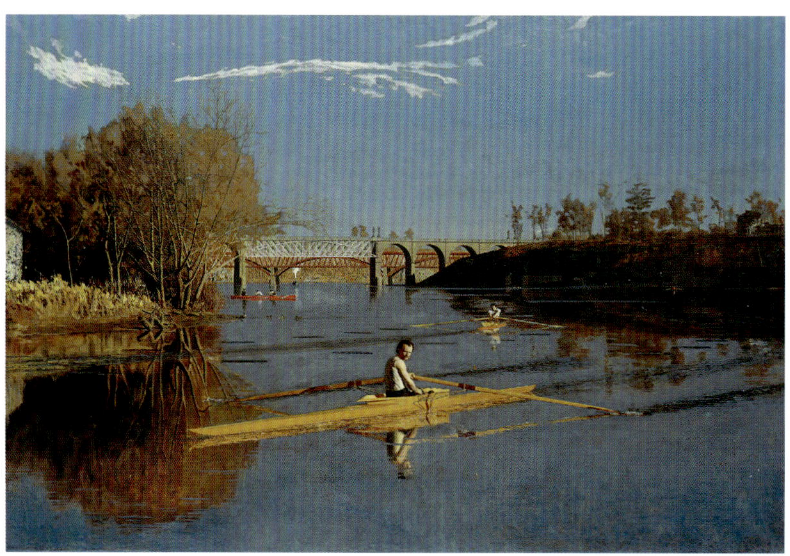

FIG. 23. Thomas Eakins (American, 1844–1916). *The Champion Single Sculls (Max Schmitt in a Single Scull)*. 1871. Oil on canvas, 32¼ x 46¼" (81.9 x 117.5 cm). THE METROPOLITAN MUSEUM OF ART, NEW YORK. PURCHASE, THE ALFRED N. PUNNETT ENDOWMENT FUND AND GEORGE D. PRATT GIFT

with which Wyeth has attended to a crow's corpse—seen in extreme close-up, each spindly, sharp talon executed with care—is frankly empathetic, almost pitying; the painting's more fanciful elements induce shivers, in particular the Brobdingnagian proportions of the crow, which dwarfs the viewer and its surroundings like a predator time-traveled from Jurassic times.

When Wyeth painted *Christina's World*, several years later, artists in postwar America were increasingly turning away from realistic and regional subject matter. Taking their cue from work by European artists who had found refuge in the United States during the war, from the geometric abstractions of Piet Mondrian to the biomorphic landscapes of Surrealists Yves Tanguy and Roberto Matta, American painters such as Franz Kline, Jackson Pollock, and Mark Tobey were developing unique ways of painting, filling canvases edge to edge with slashing calligraphic forms, skeins of dripped paint, and delicate weaves of crosshatched brushstrokes. But even as abstraction took over European and American art, Wyeth never experimented with it, and as a result, by the late 1950s critics came to consider his work academic and deeply conservative.[16] Wyeth was not ignorant of the work of his Abstract Expressionist contemporaries and spoke admiringly of the work of Kline in particular. In the same interview in which he denied any ties to realism, he professed to being "a pure abstractionist in my thought."[17]

This is perhaps not as strange as it sounds; looking closely at a Wyeth composition reveals that the artist was deeply interested in the form of the objects he painted, such as the geometry of a glass-paned window **[FIG. 26]**, the regular horizontals of clapboard evenly carving the cubic form of a saltbox house **[FIG. 27]**, even a kind of serially repetitive regularity in the grass stems that make up the field in *Christina's World*. This grass was painted over the course of several months with brushstrokes as slim as pencil lines **[FIG. 28]**. Elaine de Kooning wrote with admiration of Wyeth's controlled technique, describing how he held the paintbrush like a pencil and made his marks by moving only his fingers, steadied by the heel of his hand against the panel. She was among the first writers to point out that the meadow in the painting was not made up of thousands of individual painted blades of grass but of a density of minute strokes hatched in all directions.[18] This observation has been used to counter arguments for Wyeth's orthodoxy—his connection to minutely observed figuration—and link his technique to the calligraphic strokes of Kline or even the color fields of Mark Rothko.[19] But the freedom of his paint handling in the meadow at the center of *Christina's World*, and, indeed, in other discrete areas of landscapes he painted throughout his life, is in fact a minor detail of an artistic language overwhelmingly devoted to giving the illusion of reality. In an art world dominated by gestural abstraction and, subsequently, the techniques of mechanical reproduction used by Andy Warhol and others, Wyeth's steady and hyperrealistic hand could still be admired but increasingly seemed out-of-date. The painter Larry Rivers, something of a realist himself, albeit one with connections to both abstraction and Pop art, acknowledged as much in 1963, when he said, "Wyeth paints sonnets but no one is reading sonnets anymore."[20] Wyeth might well have been

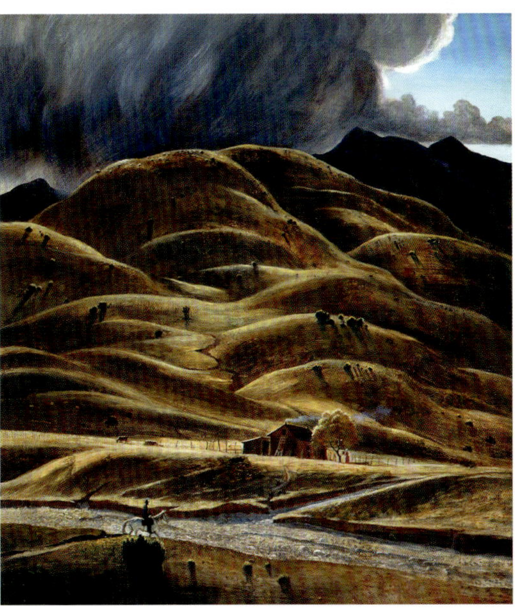

FIG. 24. Peter Hurd (American, 1904–1984). *The Dry River*. 1938. Tempera on panel, 47 x 41" (119.4 × 104.1 cm). ROSWELL MUSEUM AND ART CENTER, NEW MEXICO

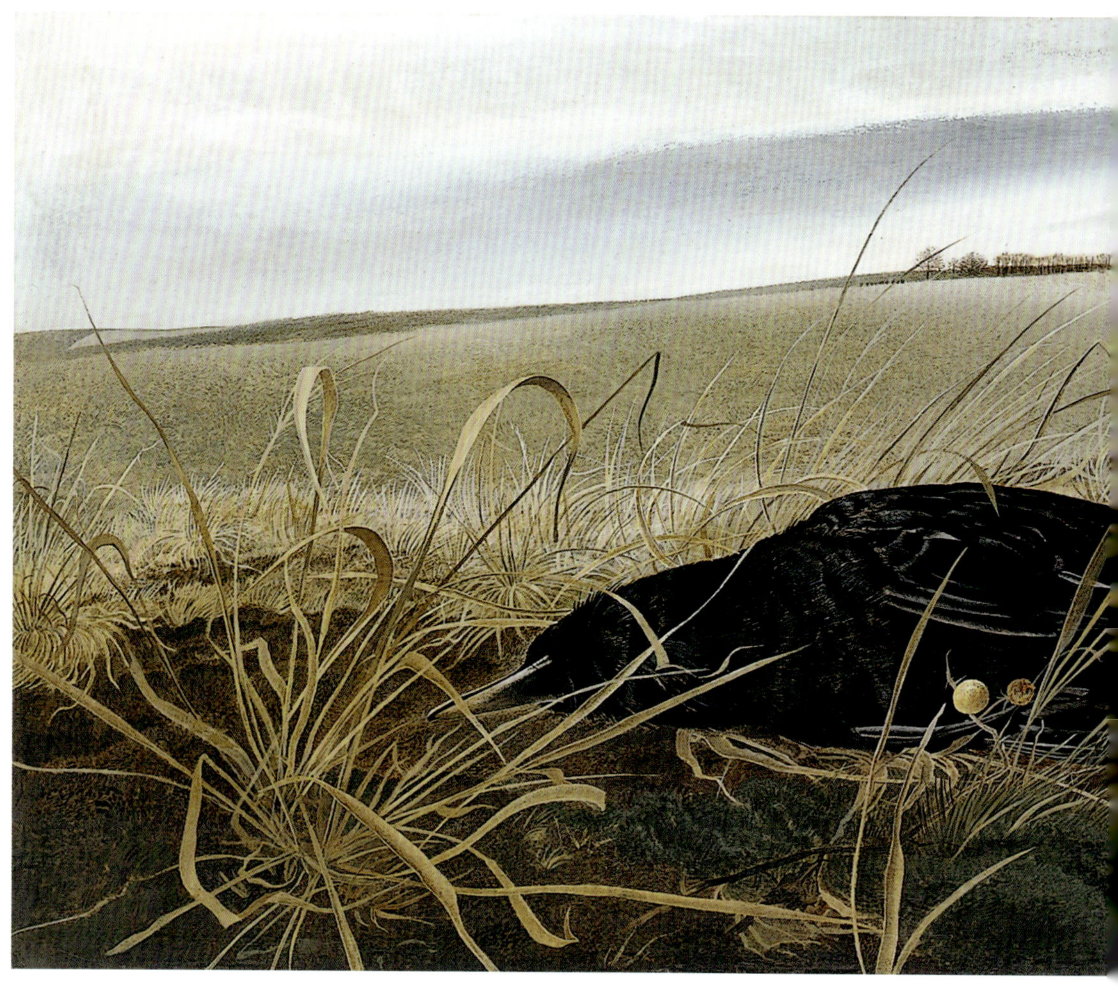

something of an abstract painter in his own mind, but by the early 1960s his work was not only seen as not modern but also universally considered a bulwark against modernism.

At the beginning of the 1950s a painter like Elaine de Kooning, associated with the New York School, could write admiringly of Wyeth, saying that he was a "master of the magic-realist technique," describing his paintings as "haunting as a train whistle in the night," and asserting that paintings like *Christina's World* demonstrated an ability to convey "the drama of loneliness curiously without pathos."[21] But compliments from the art world were rare and could not slow the widening rift between a public that deeply related to paintings like *Christina's World* and what Miller called, referring to the contemporary art world, "cultivated

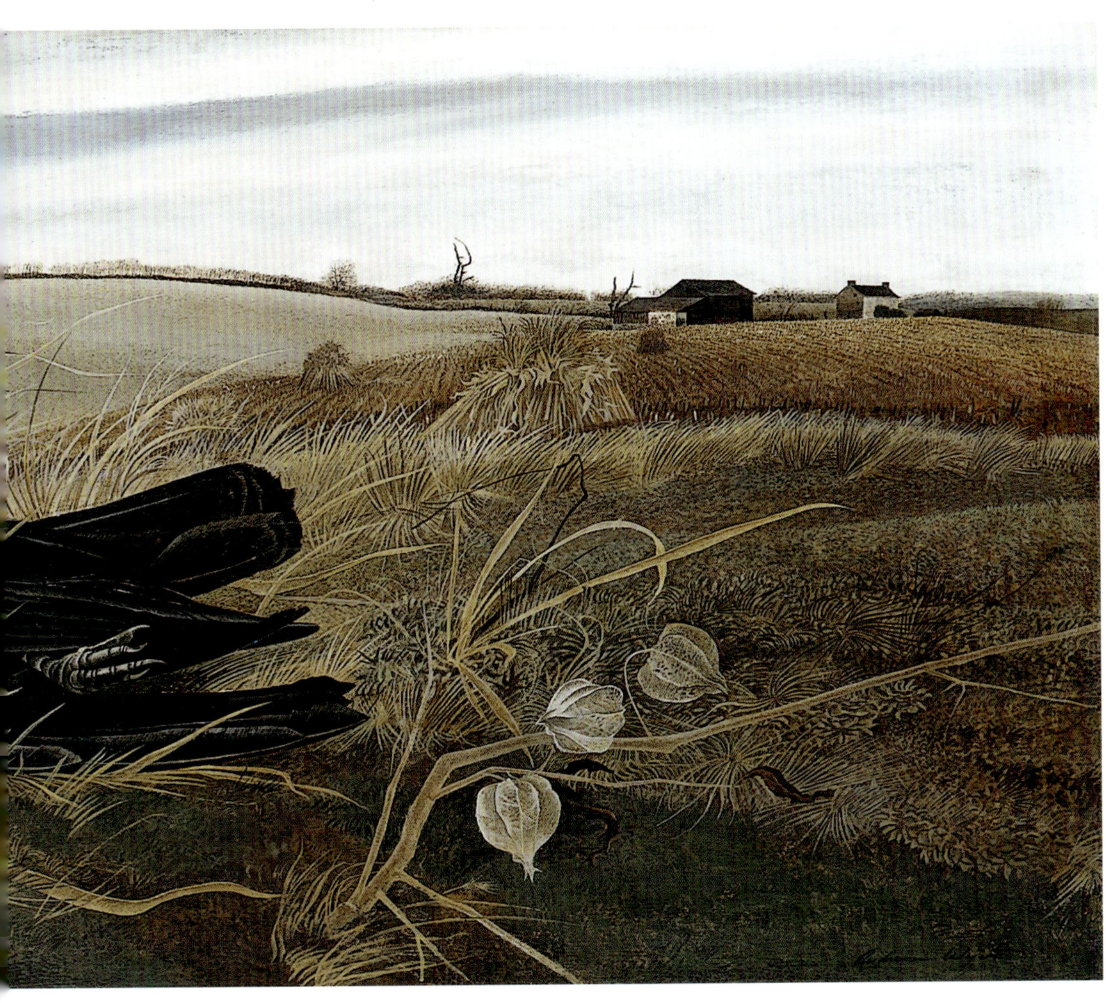

FIG. 25. Andrew Wyeth (American, 1917–2009). *Winter Fields*. 1942. Tempera on panel, 17¼ x 41" (43.8 x 104.1 cm). WHITNEY MUSEUM OF AMERICAN ART, NEW YORK. GIFT OF MR. AND MRS. BENNO C. SCHMIDT IN MEMORY OF MR. JOSIAH MARVEL, FIRST OWNER OF THIS PICTURE

taste."[22] In the 1960s the universally known and wildly popular *Christina's World* was seen by most of that art world as kitschy-anachronistic, sentimental, and too easily accessible. More important, perhaps, its endurance as an American cultural icon represented realism's hold on the aesthetic preference of everyday Americans, despite an increasing consensus among art professionals that abstraction was a more progressive and representative artistic language.

This negative critical backlash to Wyeth's success with the population at large also targeted his subjects.[23] His works are often described as snapshots of a timeless, perennially rural America, but paintings like *Christina's World* appeared at a very particular moment in American history, when the last acres of what had been a primarily rural country were disappearing and signs of modernity were

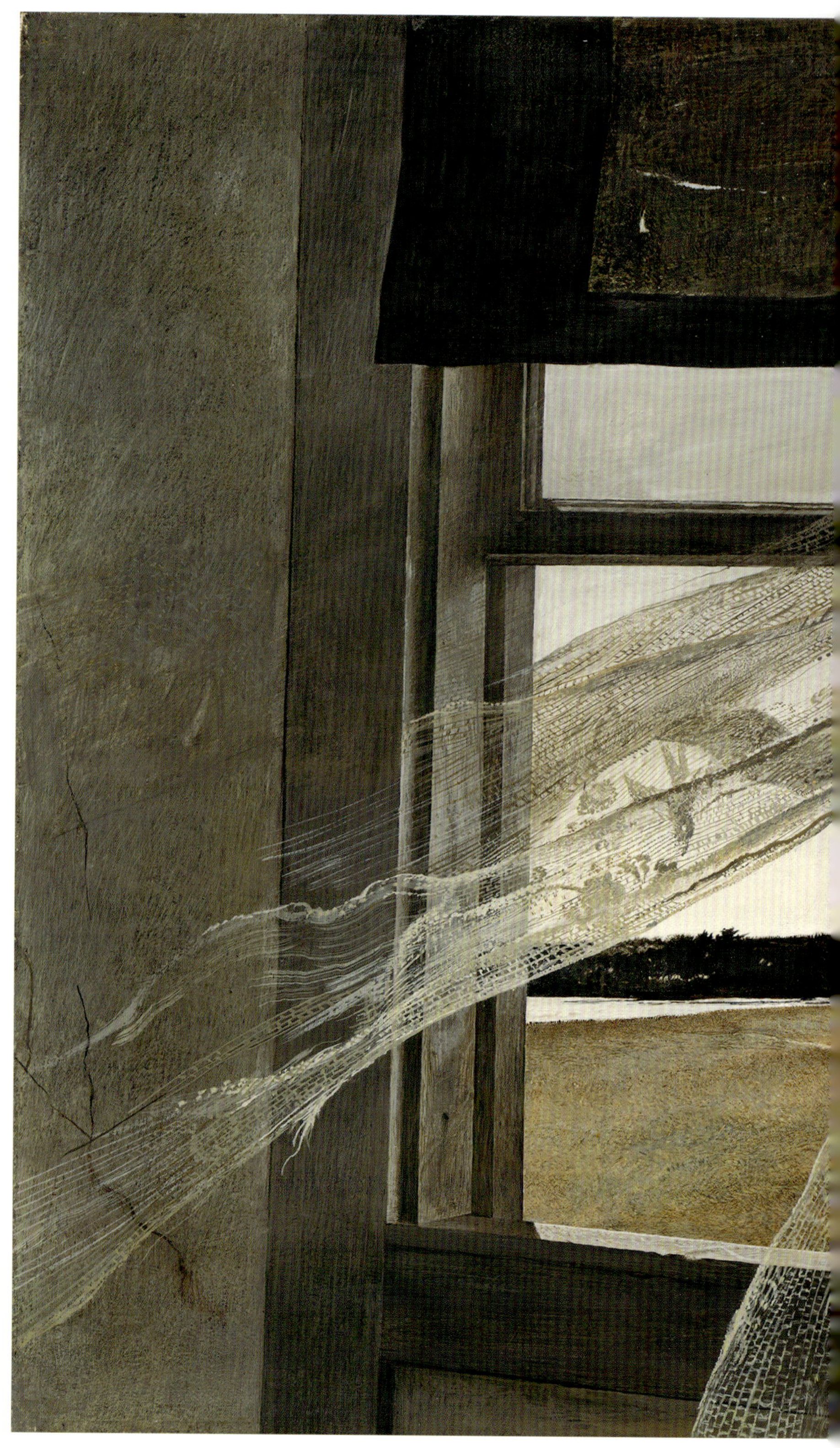

FIG. 26. Andrew Wyeth (American, 1917–2009). *Wind from the Sea*. 1947. Tempera on board, 18½ x 27$\frac{9}{16}$" (47 x 70 cm). NATIONAL GALLERY OF ART, WASHINGTON. GIFT OF CHARLES H. MORGAN

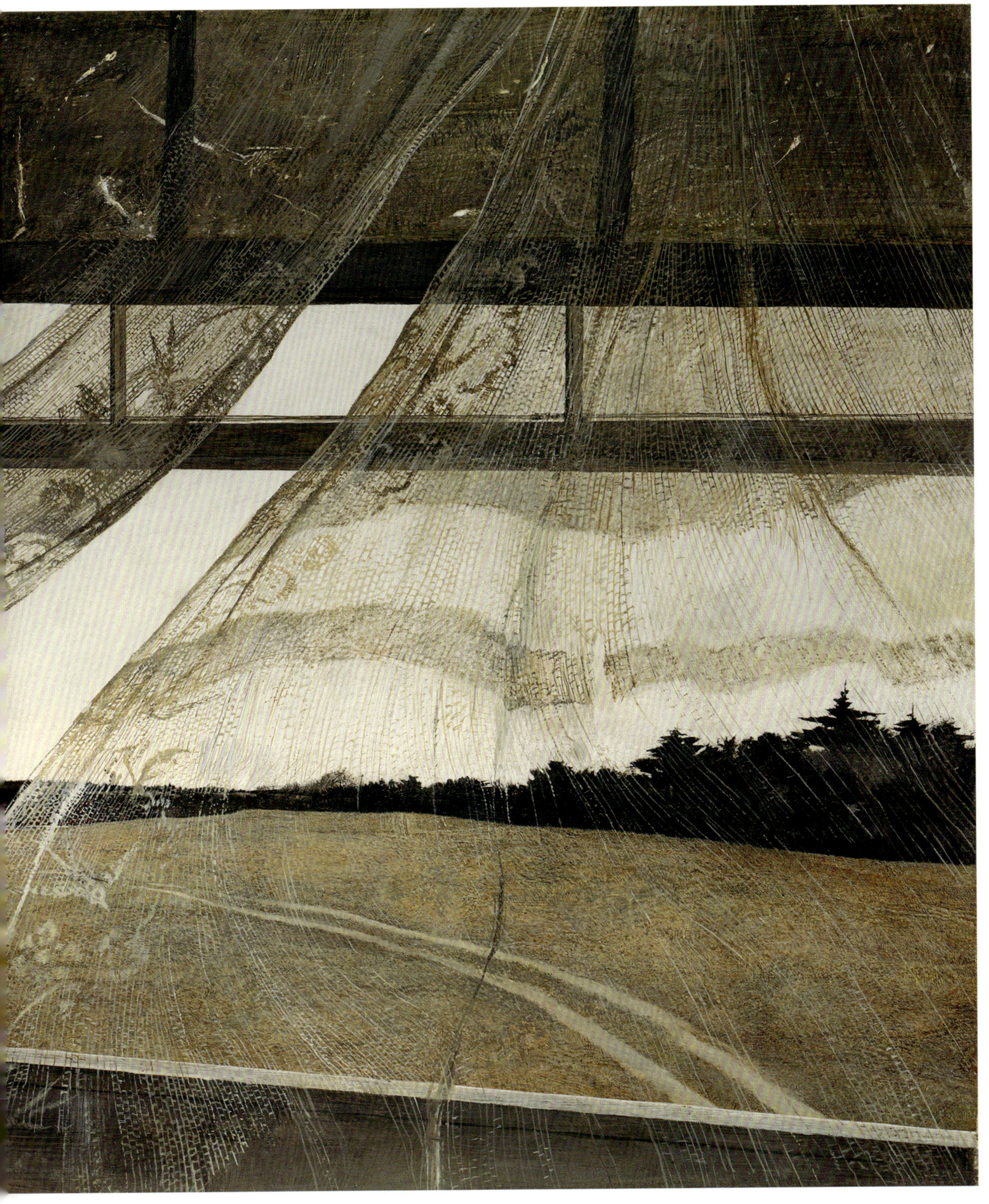

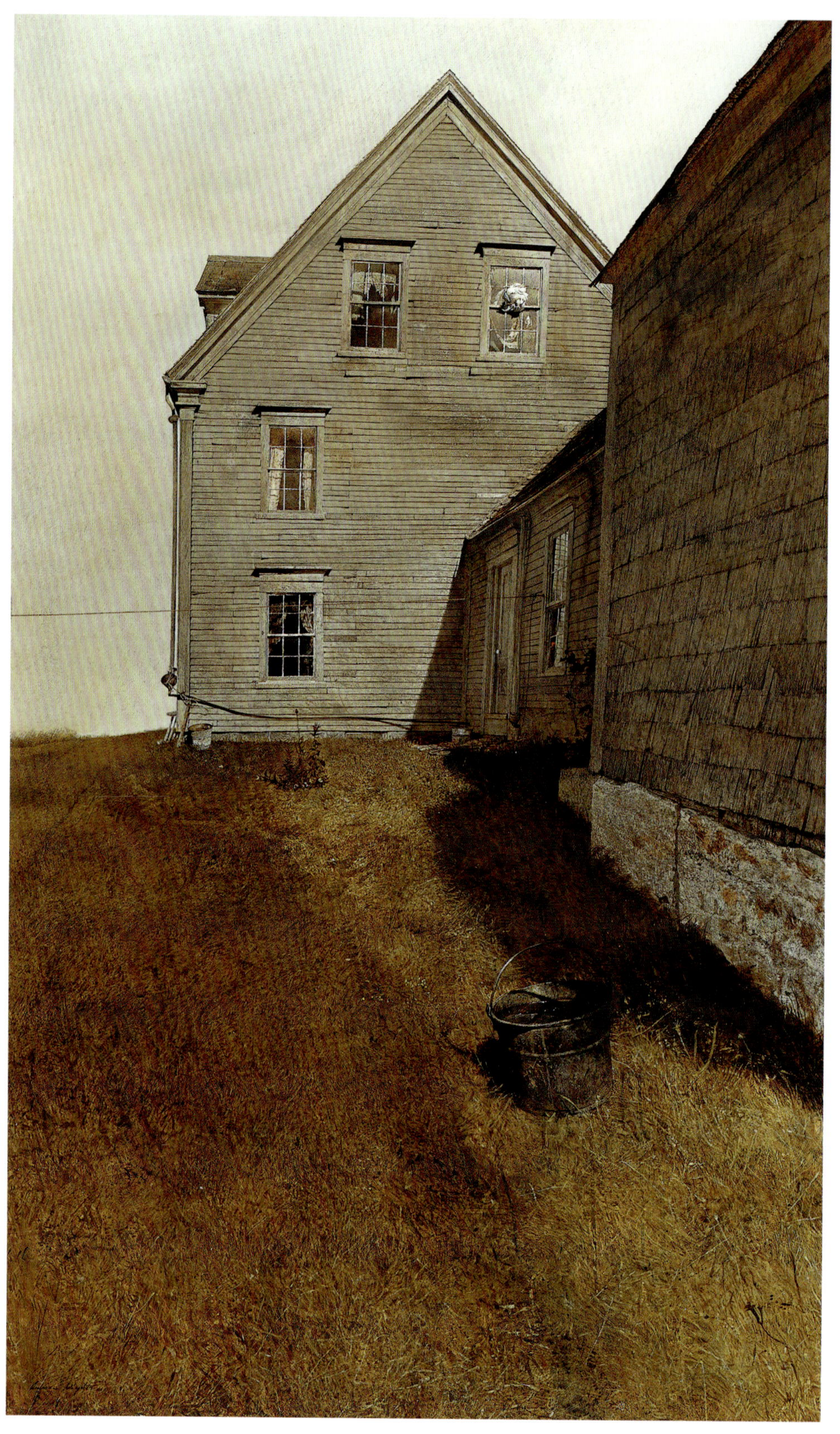

FIG. 28. Andrew Wyeth (American, 1917–2009). *Christina's World* (detail). 1948. See pp. 2–3

arriving in even the most remote byways.[24] By the beginning of the 1960s Wyeth's iconic Maine landscape could stand in for an entire American way of life that for the most part did not exist anymore: a rural, barren, hardscrabble existence far removed from the modern, televised, urban world and its bright colors and cosmopolitan crowds. His more austere America, of farm landscapes unscathed by roads or signs of industry, was inhabited by indomitable, hardworking individuals living in a poverty that was not degrading but ennobling, even picturesque. Wyeth's is not an especially bucolic vision of America, but in its radical simplicity of form and content it encouraged nostalgia for an idealized country of tough constitutions, stiff upper lips, and Puritan values, unbowed and unchanged by so-called progress.

Although Wyeth's subjects were not political, in the Cold War climate of the 1950s and '60s his paintings seemed, to some, freighted with political significance, sentimental pastiches of observed and made-up details illustrating an America that had never existed; his laserlike focus on so few subjects over such a small geographic area seemed, at best, an incuriosity about a larger world and, at worst, a celebration of a way of life that existed only in the fevered dreams of a wistful nationalist.[25] Even Wyeth's most vocal supporter, the respected art critic and ballet impresario Lincoln Kirstein, commented—although affectionately—that Wyeth "has his universe and that's it."[26] Paintings like *Christina's World* or *Young America* (1950; **FIG. 29**), which depicts a hale fellow on a bicycle

OPPOSITE: FIG. 27. Andrew Wyeth (American, 1917–2009). *Weatherside*. 1965. Tempera on panel, 48⅛ x 27⅞" (122.2 x 70.8 cm). PRIVATE COLLECTION

FIG. 29. Andrew Wyeth (American, 1917–2009). *Young America*. 1950. Tempera on board, 32½ x 45⁵⁄₁₆" (82.6 x 115.1 cm). PENNSYLVANIA ACADEMY OF THE FINE ARTS, PHILADELPHIA. JOSEPH E. TEMPLE FUND

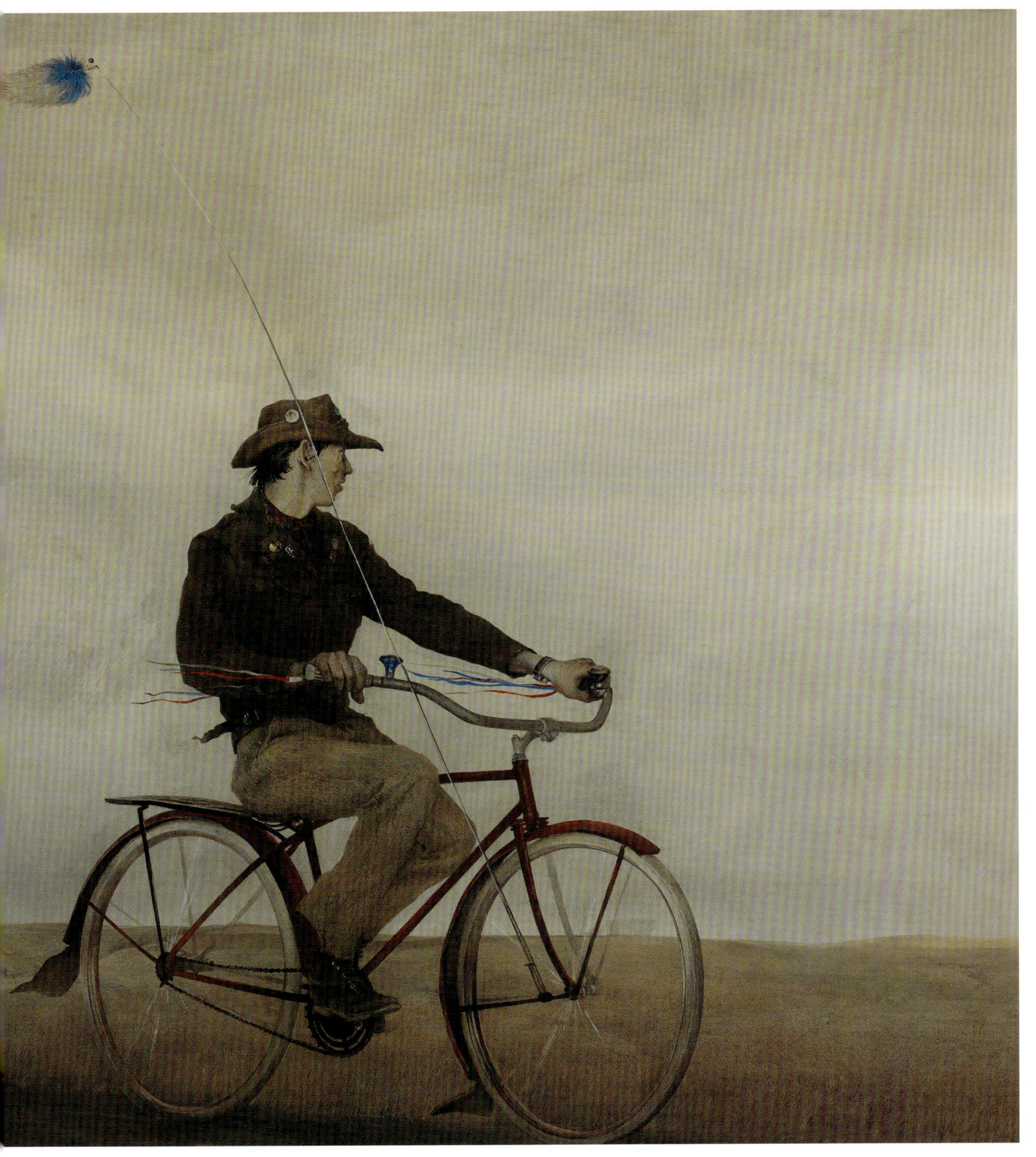

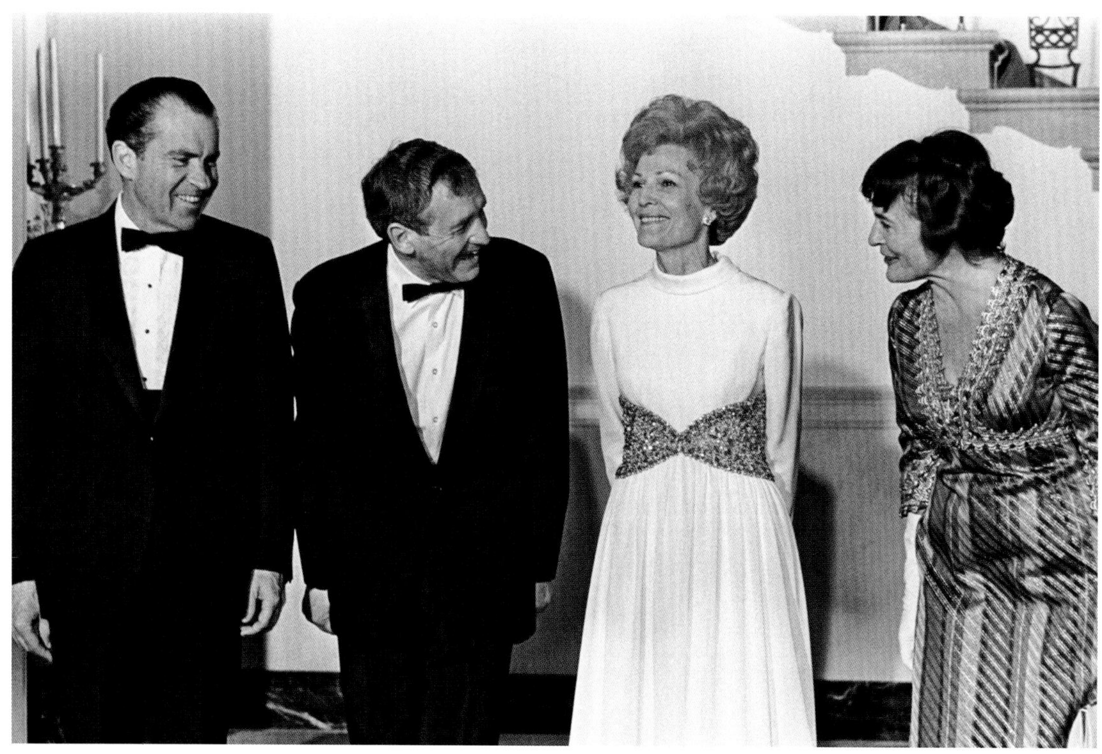

FIG. 30. President and Mrs. Nixon with Andrew and Betsy Wyeth, Washington, D.C., February 19, 1970

gaily decked out with the latest gear, appeared to some artists and critics to be aggressively provincial, an example of what the abstract painter Jack Levine called Wyeth's Americanismo.[27]

Wyeth enjoyed setting himself against what he perceived as the liberal art-world establishment that was so consistently critical of his work. In 1960 he declined an invitation to President John F. Kennedy's inaugural but visited President Richard Nixon several years later, when the White House sponsored a small solo exhibition of his work [**FIG. 30**]. He was a vocal conservative, making provocatively isolationist statements in radio, television, and newspaper interviews, to a press corps eager to use him as an example of the cultural values of the American heartland. Asked in 1963 why he had never traveled outside of the United States, Wyeth replied, "To my way of thinking, the whole future of art depends on this hemisphere. Europe has done wonderful things, but they've done it in their own way. We should do things *our* way."[28] As the representative

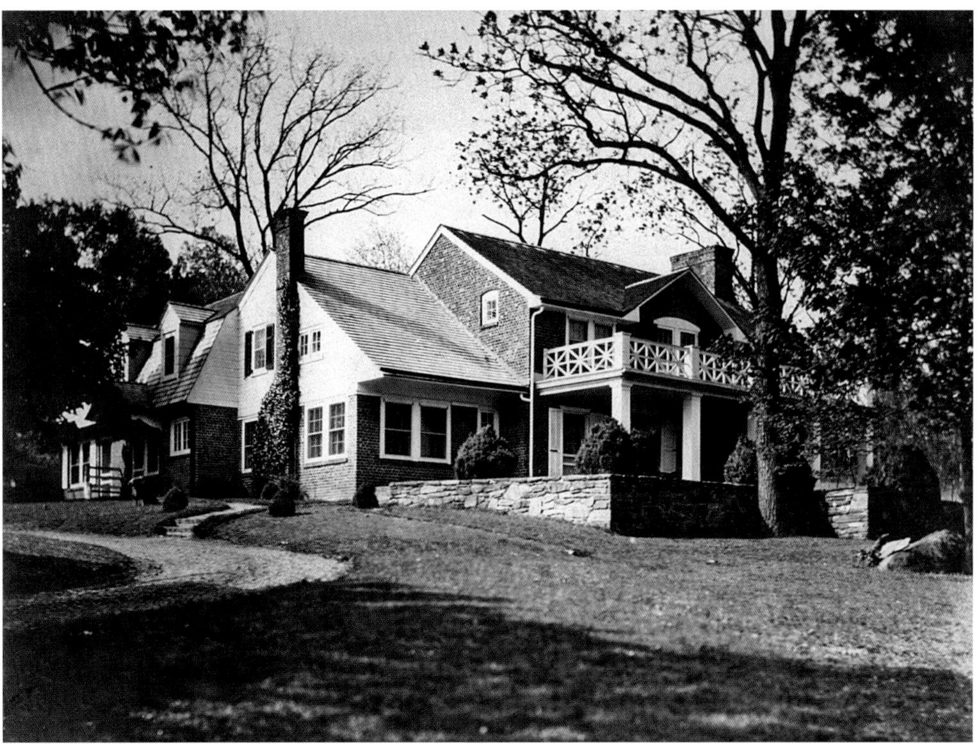

FIG. 31. The Wyeth family compound in Chadds Ford, Pennsylvania. WYETH FAMILY ARCHIVES

artist of the American people, as opposed to that of the cultural elite, Wyeth made much of living apart from the toffs of New York and Philadelphia, but at the same time he and his wife proudly displayed their lavish antibohemian lifestyle, regularly inviting journalists to their impressive compounds in Chadds Ford **[FIG. 31]** and South Cushing. In his later years he was often photographed wearing furs **[FIG. 32]**, and in 2002 he painted the interior of a private jet, with his commodious spreads in Pennsylvania and Maine visible through the windows **[FIG. 33]**.[29] This composite scene, painted more than half a century after *Christina's World*, curiously echoes the earlier painting, with its seated woman, seen from behind, gazing toward the same house that Christina did, this time with an angel's-eye view.

The gulf between professional and popular opinion of Wyeth's work has been demonstrated time and again over the years. By 1976, when Thomas Hoving, the well-known and outspoken director of New York's Metropolitan Museum of

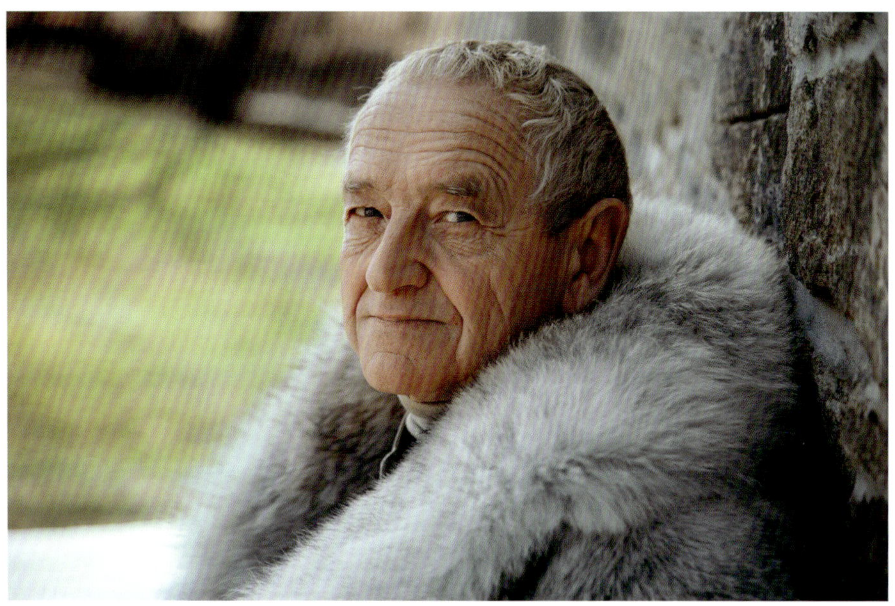

FIG. 32. Andrew Wyeth, 1983

Art, gave Wyeth a retrospective, anti-Wyeth sentiment ran high in the art world, pitting its opinion, in a rare moment of unity, against popular taste.[30] Hilton Kramer, reviewing the exhibition in the *New York Times,* wrote,

> Mr. Wyeth's vision of both art and nature is an extremely depressing one. Everything about it—the humble subjects, the provincial and weather-worn atmosphere, the implied wholesomeness and downrightness—rings false. It all seems so drained of feeling, of real observation, of any involvement with the actualities of either life or art. . . . Emerging from this phony atmosphere, how grateful one was for the sun and the crowds on Fifth Avenue![31]

Questions about the artist's sincerity and motives were raised again in 1987, when a group of more than a hundred portraits and studies, both clothed and nude, of his comely Chadds Ford neighbor Helga Testorf were exhibited at the National Gallery of Art in Washington, D.C. They were lent by a single private collector who had bought the group from Wyeth, who, along with his wife, had promoted it as a body of work heretofore unknown and never before seen. The

National Gallery—a museum that rarely devotes its galleries to the work of a living artist—hoped that in return for the exhibition and its lavish catalogue the so-called Helga paintings and drawings might remain at the museum as a gift of the owner. But immediately after the close of what turned out to be one of the biggest blockbuster exhibitions in the National Gallery's history, the collector sold the works to a Japanese investor for a reported 45 million dollars.[32] The enormous publicity generated by the Helga exhibition and subsequent scandal of the works' resale added to Wyeth's fame but also to his difficulties in the art world, and endured until the end of his life. When Wyeth died, in 2009, the *New York Times* obituary called him "one of the most popular and also most lambasted artists in the history of American art" and cited *Christina's World*, among all his works, as the one that encapsulated this double-edged renown.[33]

Both beloved and loathed since its creation almost sixty-five years ago, *Christina's World*, one of the best-known paintings in The Museum of Modern Art's collection of almost 150,000 objects, holds within it the issues that divide American culture to this day. In one critic's words this "supreme icon" for "the greater part of the American public," produced at the cusp of the flowering of abstract art in America, is "a virtual Rorschach test for American culture," pitting rural taste against urban, austerity against economic profligacy, middle-class values against intellectualism, conservative against progressive thought, and provincial notions against cosmopolitan ones.[34] Despite the controversy that surrounds it and the strong emotions it continues to elicit, *Christina's World* embodies, in an image of a young woman in a wintery field, the ideals of an America of Andrew Wyeth's creation and of countless viewers' imaginings.[35]

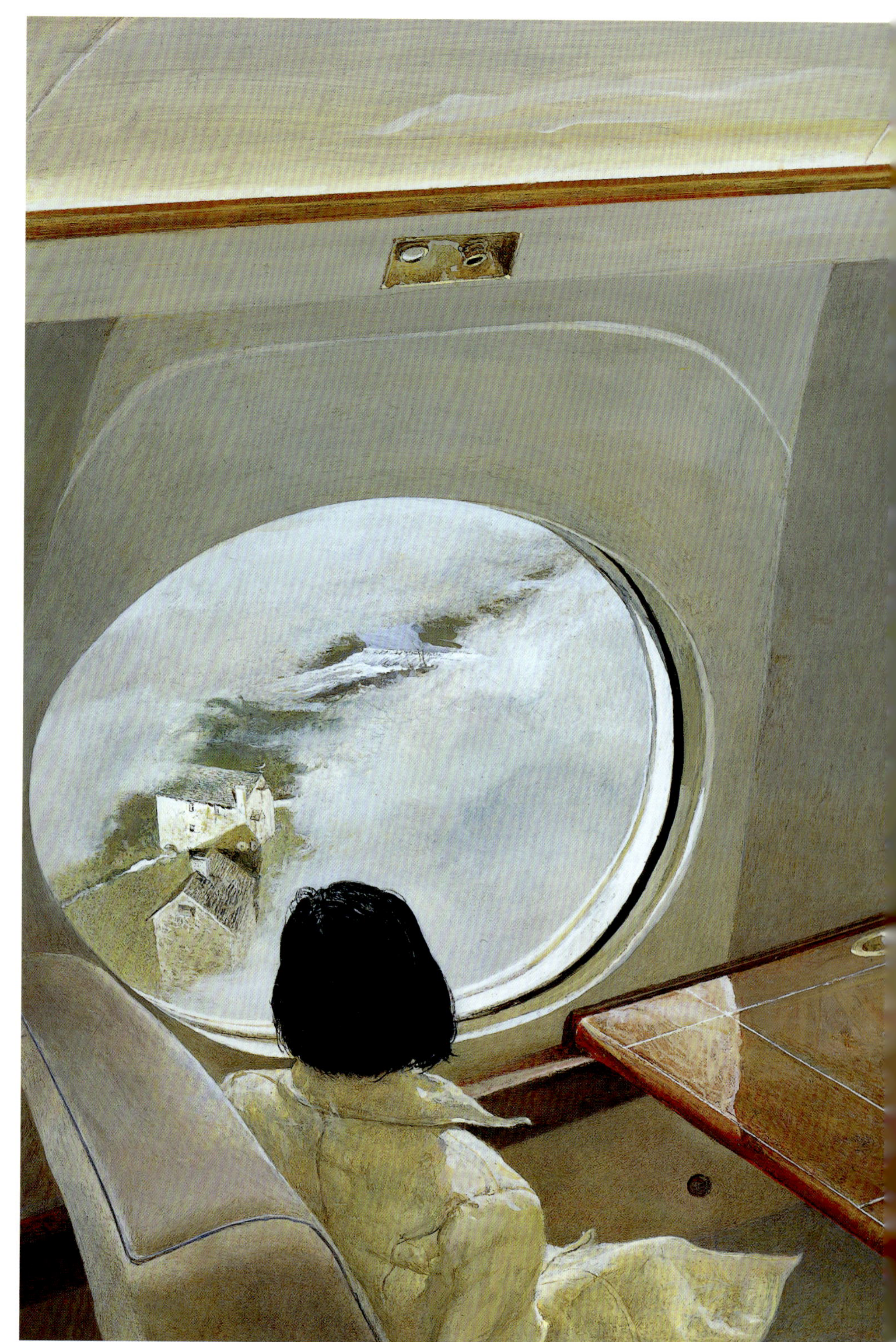

FIG. 33. Andrew Wyeth (American, 1917–2009). *Otherworld*. 2002. Tempera on panel, 30½ x 47¾" (77.5 x 121.3 cm). PRIVATE COLLECTION

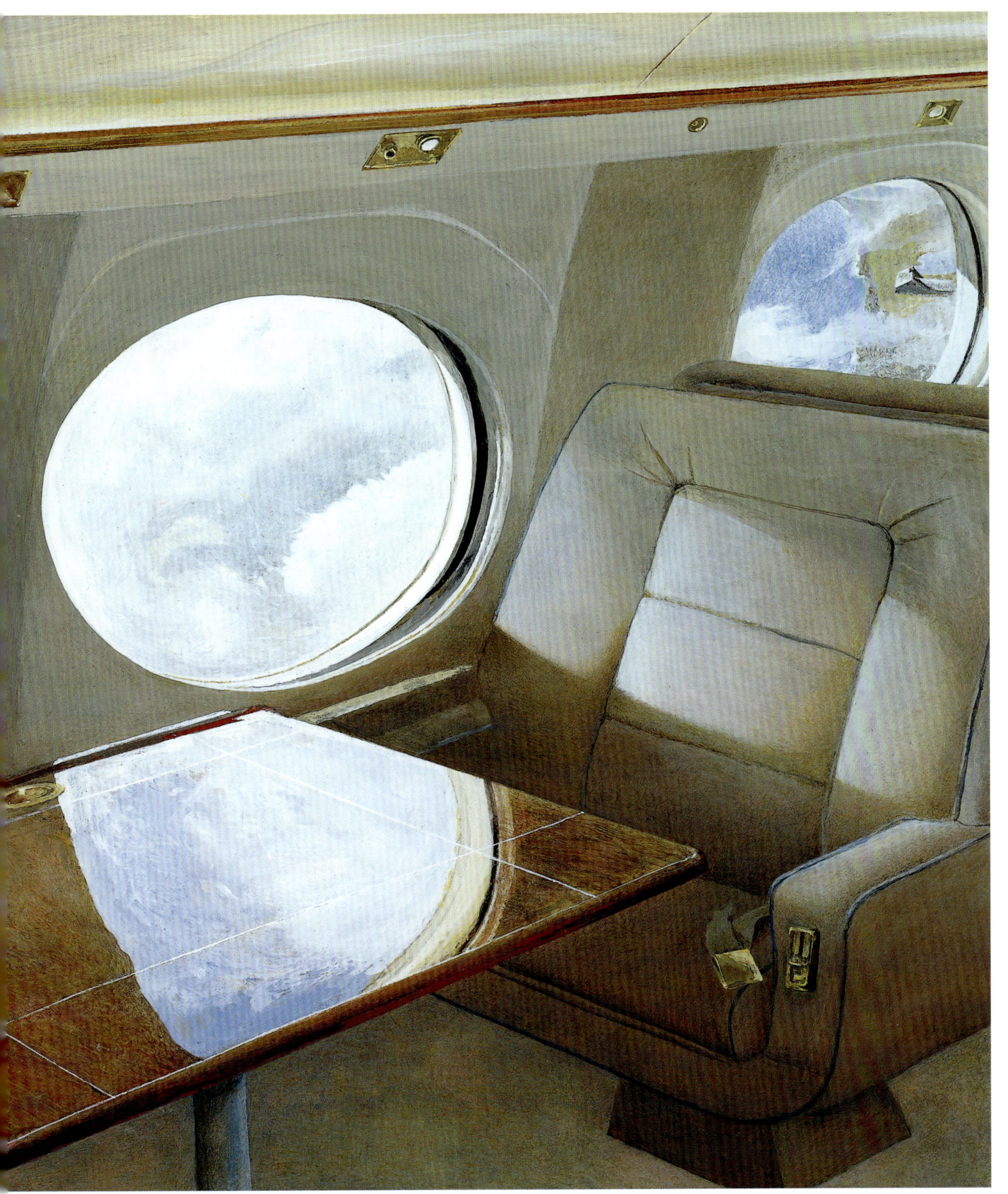

NOTES

1. Robert Rosenblum, quoted in John Gruen, "Far-from-Last Judgments or, Who's Overrated Now?," *Artnews* 76, no. 9 (November 1977): 118.

2. Almost all the literature on Andrew Wyeth begins with the claim that his popularity exceeds that of other artists. Michael Kimmelman, writing Wyeth's obituary for the *New York Times*, began with the claim that Wyeth was "one of the most popular . . . artists in the history of American art." Kimmelman, "Andrew Wyeth, Painter, Dies at 91," *New York Times*, January 16, 2009, p. A18. See also Rosenblum, "A View of Andrew Wyeth," 1987, in *On Modern American Art: Selected Essays* (New York: Harry N. Abrams, 1999), pp. 127–29; Lawrence Alloway, "The Other Andy: America's Most Popular Painter," *Arts Magazine*, April 1967, pp. 20–21; and "Andrew Wyeth: Subjective Realist," *Time*, January 7, 1957.

3. Roul Tunley, "The Wonderful World of Andrew Wyeth," *Woman's Day*, August 1963, pp. 33–37, 63–67.

4. Betsy Wyeth reported Christina's disappointment that her face was not depicted in the painting, but also that she said, "Andy put me where I wanted to be." Richard Meryman, *Andrew Wyeth: A Secret Life* (New York: Harper Collins, 1996), p. 272.

5. Wyeth, quoted in ibid., p. 20.

6. Wyeth, quoted in Kimmelman, "Andrew Wyeth, Painter, Dies at 91," p. A18; and Meryman, *Andrew Wyeth*, p. 20.

7. Wyeth, letter to Alfred H. Barr, Jr., November 1951, The Museum of Modern Art, New York, Department of Painting and Sculpture, Museum Collection Files.

8. Ibid.

9. "Models: Indomitable Vision," *Time* 91, no. 6 (February 9, 1968).

10. Wyeth, quoted in "Andrew Wyeth's World," *Time* 82, no. 26 (December 27, 1963): 44–52.

11. Dorothy C. Miller, foreword to Miller and Barr, eds., *American Realists and Magic Realists* (New York: The Museum of Modern Art, 1943), p. 7.

12. Ibid., p. 6.

13. Lincoln Kirstein, introduction to ibid., p. 8.

14. Barr, quoted in Miller, foreword to ibid., p. 5.

15. Kirstein, introduction to ibid., p. 8.

16. See George Heard Hamilton, quoted in Robert Goldwater, ed., "A Symposium: The State of American Art," *Magazine of Art* 42, no. 3 (March 1949): 93; reprinted in John L. Ward, *American Realist Painting, 1945–1980* (Ann Arbor: UMI Research Press, 1989), p. 10.

17. Wyeth, quoted in "Andrew Wyeth's World," p. 51.

18. Elaine de Kooning, "Andrew Wyeth Paints a Picture," *Artnews* 49, no. 1 (March 1950): 54.

19. John Wilmerding, introduction to *Andrew Wyeth: Memory and Magic* (New York: Rizzoli, 2005), p 20.

20. Larry Rivers's work was deeply engaged with the history of American realist painting. His best-known painting is a modernist version of Emanuel Leutz's iconic nineteenth-century masterpiece *Washington Crossing the Delaware* (1851), completed in 1953. Rivers, quoted in "Andrew Wyeth's World," p. 52.

21. De Kooning, "Andrew Wyeth Paints a Picture," p. 36.

22. Miller, foreword to Miller and Barr, eds., *American Realists and Magic Realists*, p. 2.

23. The art critic and artist Brian O'Dougherty wrote with great feeling in 1974 about the modernist backlash against Wyeth's work: "Modern art is urban art. While it accepts the urban view of the landscape . . . it will not accept the rural view, nor is it equipped to read it, or perceive it in anything more than the clichés identified with forms of nationalism troubling to the liberal spirit. . . . Thus, Wyeth, the only genuine rural artist of the slightest consequence, is attacked with a violence far beyond the visual etiquette of critical disagreement." O'Dougherty, quoted in Meryman, *Andrew Wyeth*, p. 397.

24. "Andrew Wyeth's World," p. 52.

25. See Alloway, "The Other Andy," pp. 20–21; and John Canaday, "Wyeth: His Nostalgia for a Vanished America Is Still a Best Seller," *New York Times*, July 26, 1970, among others.

26. Kirstein, quoted in Kimmelman, "An Imperfect American Idol and His Self-Enclosed Art," *New York Times*, January 17, 1997.

27. "Andrew Wyeth's World," p. 52.

28. Wyeth, quoted in Tunley, "The Wonderful World of Andrew Wyeth," p. 68.

29. The coat he was photographed in was in fact made of less-than-lavish coyote fur.

30. Thomas Hoving, the director of The Metropolitan Museum, New York, from 1967 to 1977, was known for his zeal in bringing general audiences to art museums.

31. Hilton Kramer, "Mammoth Wyeth Exhibition at Met," *New York Times*, October 16, 1976.

32. Ralph Blumenthal "Still Sovereign of His Own Art," *New York Times*, February 18, 1997, p. C11.

33. Kimmelman, "Andrew Wyeth, Painter, Dies at 91," p. A1.

34. Rosenblum, "A View of Andrew Wyeth," p. 127

35. Ibid.

FOR FURTHER READING

ON ANDREW WYETH

Corn, Wanda M. *The Art of Andrew Wyeth* (Greenwich, Conn.: New York Graphic Society, 1973).

Knutson, Anne Classen, et. al. *Andrew Wyeth: Memory and Magic* (Atlanta: High Museum of Art; Philadelphia: Philadelphia Museum of Art, in association with Rizzoli, New York, 2005).

Meryman, Richard. *Andrew Wyeth: A Secret Life* (New York: Harper Collins, 1996).

Wyeth, Betsy James. *Christina's World* (Boston: Houghton Mifflin, 1982).

ON AMERICAN REALISM

Lucie-Smith, Edward. *American Realism* (New York: Harry N. Abrams, 1994).

Rosenblum, Robert. *On Modern American Art: Selected Essays by Robert Rosenblum* (New York: Harry N. Abrams, 1999).

Ward, John L. *American Realist Painting, 1945–1980* (Ann Arbor: UMI Research Press, 1989).

Produced by The Department of Publications
The Museum of Modern Art, New York

Edited by Emily Hall
Designed by Miko McGinty and Rita Jules
Production by Matthew Pimm
Printed and bound by Oceanic Graphic Printing, Inc., China

Typeset in Ideal Sans
Printed on 157 gsm Gold East Matte Artpaper

Library of Congress Control Number: 2012935388
ISBN: 978-0-87070-831-2

Published by The Museum of Modern Art
11 West 53 Street
New York, New York 10019-5497
www.moma.org

Distributed in the United States and Canada by ARTBOOK | D.A.P.,
155 Sixth Avenue, 2nd floor, New York, New York 10013
www.artbook.com

Distributed outside the United States and Canada by Thames & Hudson Ltd.,
181A High Holborn, London WC1V 7QX
www.thamesandhudson.com

Printed in China

PHOTOGRAPH CREDITS

In reproducing the images contained in this publication, the Museum obtained the permission of the rights holders whenever possible. If the Museum could not locate the rights holders, notwithstanding good-faith efforts, it requests that any contact information concerning such rights holders be forwarded so that they may be contacted for future editions.

All works by Andrew Wyeth © 2012 Andrew Wyeth

© Figge Art Museum, successors to the Estate of Nan Wood Graham/Licensed by VAGA, New York, NY: 4 (right)

© Albertina, Vienna, Inv. 3073: 19. © The Art Institute of Chicago, 1930.934: 4 (right). Sheldon C. Collins: 30–31. © Wally McNamee/CORBIS: 38. © The Metropolitan Museum of Art/Art Resource, NY: 27. Department of Imaging Services, The Museum of Modern Art, New York: 2-3, 5, 24, 35; photo by Thomas Griesel: 26. Courtesy the National Gallery of Art, Washington: 32. New Britain Museum of American Art, 1953.18: 18. Peter Ralston: 22. © Réunion des Musées Nationaux/Art Resource, NY, Jean-Gilles Berizzi: 4 (left). © Richard Schulman/CORBIS: 40. Kosti Ruohomaa-Black Star: 15

TRUSTEES OF THE MUSEUM OF MODERN ART